From Hardened to Healed

The Effortless Path to Release Resistance, Get Unstuck, and Create a Life You Love
©2021

by Dr. Debi Silber

D0746331

From Hardened to Healed

The Effortless Path to Release Resistance,
Get Unstuck, and Create a Life You Love

Published by The PBT Institute

125 Newtown Road, Plainview, New York 11803

thepbtinstitute.com

Debi@PBTInstitute.com

Copyright © 2021 By Dr. Debi Silber

All rights reserved. No part of this book may be reproduced in any form or by any electronic or mechanical means, including information storage and retrieval systems, without written permission from the publisher, except by a reviewer who may quote passages in a review.

Names: Silber, Debi, author

Title: From Hardened to Healed: the effortless path to release resistance, get unstuck, and

create a life you love / Debi Silber

Description: The PBT Institute, [2021] / Summary: "Some of us will go through one or more traumatic experiences. Others may simply have a negative belief system that's created a sense of fear, uncertainty, scarcity, and lack. It's not that these experiences happen to us that's the problem; it's what we do with them. They can make us bitter and resentful, or they can help us become healed and transformed. Have your experiences left you healed … or hardened? Through From Hardened to Healed: The Effortless Path to Release Resistance, Get Unstuck, and Create a Life You Love, you'll be guided to move through Dr. Debi Silber's proven and predictable research-based steps, so you can create the health, work, relationships, and life you want most. In her practical and inspiring way, she'll help you "face it and feel it, so you can heal it." No matter where you are on the 'healed-or-hardened spectrum,' the good news is, the tools you need for your transformation are here for you inside this book."—Provided by publisher.

ISBN 978-1-7378457-0-6

Library of Congress Control Number: 2021919475

Other books by Dr. Debi Silber:

Trust Again: Overcoming Betrayal and Regaining Health, Confidence and Happiness (Silber; 2020)

The Unshakable Woman (Silber; 2017)

The Unshakable Woman: The Workbook (Silber; 2017)

A Pocket Full of Mojo: 365 Proven Strategies to Create Your Ultimate Body, Mind, Image and Lifestyle (Silber; 2014)

Dr. Debi Silber

Contents

Dedication

This book is dedicated to those who are ready for more.

To those who are willing to get uncomfortable in order to live a life of purpose, meaning, and fulfillment.

To those who are ready to listen to that soft voice and gentle nudge urging them to take that next step ... even when they don't know what it will lead to.

I believe in you, and I believe in your greatness.

It's your time.

This Book Is Also Dedicated ...

To the brave warriors found within The PBT Institute: I'm in awe of your strength and determination to heal.

To our incredible Certified PBT Coaches and Practitioners: I'm honored and grateful that you've chosen to serve our Community with your brilliant skills and talents.

To Team PBT: Our one-of-a-kind Community would only be a dream if I didn't have your wisdom and support. I'm so grateful for your trust in this mission.

To my brilliant coaches and mentors: You inspire me to play bigger and help me share my heart with the world.

To my amazing friends, mastermind buddies, BOD, and Pow—wow!: I'm blessed to be able to spend time, brainstorm, collaborate, and learn with you all.

To my family: I love you with all my heart. You are my world.

Foreword

I had only started reading **Trust Again: Overcoming Betrayal and Regaining Health, Confidence, and Happiness** by my good friend Dr. Debi Silber when I got a chill and had to put down the book and take a deep breath. Part of my own "operating system" had just been cracked. I finally had a cogent explanation for why I approached (and avoided) certain business and personal relationships the way I did. If I had only met Debi 20 years earlier, how different my life might have been. Fortunately for me, I now had the tools and strategies to make the rest of my years the best of my years. My wiring wasn't permanent. New circuits could be created, and I really could script a new journey ... different from the one I was on.

Being a typical "dude," it had never dawned on me that my own triggers, reactions, risk tolerance, and stress response had been shaped by betrayal, but there I was, both shocked and relieved that Debi had connected the dots for me in a way that no one did before. The ex-wife I found cheating, the business partner who ousted me from the company I created, the friend who really didn't have my back, even the contractors and vendors who failed to deliver what was promised had each played some role in shaping who I had become and how I related to others.

While that surprised me, these kinds of revelations don't surprise Debi. She's always connecting the dots, figuring out the links between cause and effect. If there was anything she wanted or needed, Debi developed a plan to achieve it, whether in her personal or professional life—and she took action. But it took more than resilience. It took decoupling triggers and responses.

In her newest book, **From Hardened to Healed,** Debi has taken the methods she developed and refined within The PBT Institute and created an easy-to-follow roadmap that breaks down the process of going from hardened, cynical, and hurt by betrayal to healed, happy, and enjoying a much easier life free of the pain caused by past trauma. Her simple, relatable framework and easily actionable steps make it possible to finally decouple from a past betrayal and the pain it causes, so we can experience the joy that occurs when we are free to embrace and look forward to the future.

Debi's unstoppable drive to always find the path forward, coupled with a never-ending desire to help others find their own freedom from betrayal, has ended needless pain and suffering for thousands of women (and men) who now have their best years ahead of them, enjoying each day with renewed optimism.

In my own life, whenever I am looking for a guide, someone who can help me navigate something new or difficult, I look for a coach who understands what I'm working through and has taken the journey I'm on—someone who can explain things in an easily relatable way and give me the essential few steps I need to take, one at a time, to make measurable progress. This is Debi's superpower. There really is nobody better at helping people who've been hurt by betrayal break free from their past trauma.

If you feel stuck, like you're on a "hamster wheel" of never-ending trauma that creates unnecessary stress in your life, but you still dream of enjoying more carefree days—those when waking up naturally puts a smile on your face, and the people in your life are the BEST part of each day … you've found the right guide and picked up the right book. Close your eyes, take a deep breath, imagine what your ideal life looks like, feels like, smells like, and sounds like, and hold that thought for a moment. Then, turn the page to begin the journey from hardened to healed. - Karl Krummenacher, *Chief Executive Officer*, **Mindshare Collaborative**

✗ People who want me in their life - not because they need me -- they just love me & want the true, genuine, God created, freu loving, caring, Lord loving, creative, joyfull Angie).

✗ Time for people & play
✗ Work that fulfills & provides enough.
✗ Good health - feel good & right "in the middle".

a life filled with love, meaning & significance

INTRODUCTION
Healed or hardened? Where do you stand in the aftermath of your experience?

I remember watching an interview with someone who'd overcome many challenges early in life: an abusive and alcoholic parent, bullying, changing locations so often that whenever friendships would develop, it would be time to move again, poverty, and more. A pervasive sense of not belonging coupled with never knowing when the next beating would come left this person with lots to heal from …. and they did. These early childhood experiences served as fuel for a few things: physical strength to fight back if/when necessary, mental strength to skillfully create a future with little resemblance to the past, and financial security to create a sense of safety.

Most people may have watched the interview thinking, "Wow, they've come so far; look what they've been able to overcome," and by anyone's standards, they certainly had. Something didn't feel right to me, however, and while yes, this person *had* overcome insurmountable odds, I was struck by what *wasn't* being said. It was rather conveyed by their responses, the way they were sitting, and the energy they were exuding. It was unmistakable in the way they spoke and in what felt like the motivation to create all they had now. It was so powerful, I even said it out loud:

"This person isn't healed. They're hardened."

I was shocked by my own words, and that unmistakable knowing gave me goosebumps. Whenever the goosebumps show up, it's my way of knowing I'm onto something. That same feeling served as the inspiration for my previous books, programs, and **The PBT Institute**. And it's the inspiration behind this book you're reading right now.

The more I explored this idea of being either healed or hardened, the more I realized how many of us fall within varying degrees on the "healed-or-hardened spectrum." What does it mean to be healed? What does it mean to be hardened? More importantly, why should you care?

A few reasons. First, you're here to live a life filled with love, meaning, and significance. I've found that challenges in the past often serve as the best motivators to create lives rich and meaningful as a result. When we view those same experiences as reasons to close ourselves off to intimacy, trust, and the potential to create fulfilling experiences, it's a wasted opportunity. What's worse is that when we don't use our experiences, painful or otherwise, to open our minds and hearts, we often become bitter and resentful. Sure, we're never going to allow that painful experience to happen again, but we've closed ourselves off to what could bring us so much joy in the process.

Next, when we heal enough to feel like we're standing on solid ground again and then plant roots there, we prevent ourselves from healing further. This is the place where we resign ourselves to thinking, "This is as good as it's going to get, so I'd better get used to it." That belief cements you to that spot, preventing you from the healing and transformation waiting for you when you continue to move forward. Stay there for too long, and over time, it feels impossible to imagine being, doing, or having anything other than what you currently experience.

Finally, trauma is the setup for transformation. If you've been through hardship, you're already primed for a version of yourself who'd blow your mind if you allowed the transformation process to unfold. To get there, however, isn't always graceful, neat, or pretty. It can be grueling, uncomfortable, messy, and unfamiliar, which are often reasons we justify staying exactly where we are.

So, if you've already been through the hardest part of the journey anyway, why not move through all of it, so there are no remnants or imprints tattooed on your heart? Sure, there may be a few scars that serve as reminders, but wouldn't it feel better to see a reminder of all you've overcome versus a reminder that triggers more anger or pain?

So what's the difference between being healed and being hardened? How do you know where you stand and what can you do about it?

That's what this book is all about.

There's a saying we use within **The PBT (Post Betrayal Transformation) Institute**, and it's the way we teach our members to fully move through their experience: "Face it; feel it; heal it." We say that because we need to face the challenge or obstacle that's holding us back and in need of our attention. Once we face it, we need to feel it. We can't ignore the emotions and feelings that need to be uncovered and expressed. They need to be processed and allowed the space to be felt. When they're denied, ignored, or squelched, they get stuck within the body. Once they do, they run a painful subconscious program based on what they're trying to say, and they create dis-ease within our bodies. So, once we've faced it and felt it, then we need to heal it. When we see what needs our attention, then acknowledge the feelings and emotions being generated as a result of the experience, it's then time to process those emotions fully, so we heal.

I see countless people getting stuck because they don't fully move through all three of these stages. They may choose to ignore something, and when they do, they don't face what needs their attention. Or, they may face something, but when those uncomfortable feelings arise when they think about it, they'll grab a drink, reach for the cookies, or numb out in front of the TV in order to squelch what those feelings are trying to get across. Or, some people face it and feel it, but then they get stuck in a face-it-feel-it loop, where they go over their painful experience countless times, generating the anger, pain, hurt, sadness, etc. without coming out of it feeling any better than they did when they first thought about it. They do this over and over and over again. This is where we dig a hole so deep, we can't seem to find a way out of it. You think about what happened (an event, painful conversation, etc.), conjure up all the feelings that go along with it, keep thinking about it, generate more painful feelings, and repeat—it's an endless loop that goes nowhere.

Instead, what we'll be doing here is going through all three phases:

1. Face it (so you know what you're working with).

2. Feel it (so you have a clear handle on the emotions generated that need to be processed).

3. Heal it (so you can implement an action plan to do something good with it … once and for all).

That's why this book is broken down into three sections.

PART ONE: Face It: This is all about seeing where you are on the healed-or-hardened spectrum. We'll be diving into how common it is to have our experiences leave us hardened and how to know if that's where you are. We'll dive into what hardened people do, how they think, how they act, and how their habits and behaviors create more of the same. You'll see how numbing, avoiding, and distracting yourself may have been what you chose to do in order to avoid discomfort, what it's created, and what it's keeping you from now. The best part is, once you see what it's holding you back from, you'll be inspired toward change.

Let's be clear, though: you may not be in a bad place at all. You may even be looking, feeling, and living pretty well. That's great, if you feel happy and fulfilled. But if there's something left untapped, issues left unresolved, or areas needing attention, why not clean that up?

As we dive deeper, we'll explore who you'd be if you allowed yourself a new way to think and feel—if you were willing to let go of protection you no longer need. We'll dive into the fear, the risk, and reward of vulnerability, and why it's so hard yet opens the door to so much.

We'll also explore what healing looks like, along with steps to move you toward greater healing, what healed people do, how they feel, and how they think.

PART TWO: Feel It: Once you know what healed and hardened looks like, what feelings and emotions are left in the clean-up of your experience? If you dealt with the sadness, pain, sense of unworthiness, insecurity, or negative belief system created by those beliefs, who would you be? What would it feel like to have a different perspective around the experience ... one where you can see it through a lens that felt less angry or scarce, and instead felt more open and compassionate?

Now, let's talk about change for a minute, because right now, you might be feeling that this is a long and grueling process. Not at all. People think that change takes time. I disagree. Yes, the results take time to see, but the decision is what ignites the fire and puts things in motion. That change begins the minute you make the decision to change. Here's where you'll process the emotions that have been keeping you either sick, small, or stuck, and make a decision and commit to who you want to become. I'll provide the fuel you need to help get you there.

PART THREE: Heal It: I give you all the tools and support you need to apply what you've learned in order to move you toward a more healed state. Here's where we put ideas into action and strategically create a plan to slowly and steadily move you forward. You'll move toward a version of you that no longer has the same need for all that protection as you become someone who's ready to engage more fully in life and all it has to offer.

As you make changes and come through the other side of your experience, you'll have an opportunity to look back and see how far you've come. This is where you'll be inspired to share your story, pay it forward, and start something new based on what you can see so clearly now. Here's where it gets really fun—we'll take the time to celebrate! Why? Because we're so good at saying what we stink at, yet we often need to remind ourselves of the changes we've made and the road we've traveled. Of course, I'll be keeping it practical, too, with steps and tools to keep you focused and on track.

So, here's what I invite you to do as you move through these three sections:

Come to it with an open mind (which you already have, or you wouldn't have added this book to your collection in the first place).

Consider the possibility that maybe there's another way—that's not to suggest that I have the perfect solution for you at all. It's merely to suggest that if something is missing in your life, consider the possibility that, with a few new ideas, you may be open and more receptive to seek and pursue what could be your next best steps.

Check in. Once you identify who you've been and how you've been showing up and consider the possibility that there might be more, the next step is to check in with your resistance. Are you the type to have your arms crossed over your chest, head tilted a bit to the side, with the attitude of "Prove it to me"?

Are you feeling that you're going to need to move past yourself to get to your best self?

Do you realize that you're doing a great job, and there's so much to be proud of, but if you're completely honest with yourself, there are a few nagging challenges you've been putting off working on with the hope that they'll go away on their own?

Do you spend your day in joy, bliss, curiosity, compassion, and love? And while life is filled with joy and fulfillment, your curious mind wants to be sure nothing is left untapped in this one beautiful life you're living now?

Create. Here's where we're going to create a roadmap to move from hardened to healed. Everything begins with awareness, so this is where we create our plan. Once you've become aware of how you're showing up, are willing to see if you've settled in some areas of life that are important to you, and have checked in with your resistance to see how willing you are to change a few things, it's time to get moving.

What's the point of identifying blocks and not doing anything about them? That seems like a complete waste of time, and I know you don't have time to waste. So, we're going to address all those blocks, see why they're there, and what's been keeping them firmly in place, so we can strategically move past each one. When you do, you move from resistance to willingness, and hardened to healed.

So, now that you know where we're headed, are you ready? I'll meet you in PART ONE.

12/23/21   Bloodwork Done 8825
           Meet w/ Kristen   200

PART ONE
Face It

"We must be willing to get rid of the life we've planned,
so as to have the life that is waiting for us.
The old skin has to be shed before the new one can come.
If we fix on the old, we get stuck. When we hang onto any form,
we are in danger of putrefaction.
Hell is life drying up."
- Joseph Campbell

A Few Definitions and Examples

When I'm talking about being "healed or hardened," what do I mean? Let's start with a few definitions.

According to the Merriam-Webster dictionary, "hardened" is to confirm in disposition, feelings, or actions. To be hardened is to make callous and to toughen[1].

For our purposes, it doesn't necessarily mean you're angry or bitter. It can mean that old baggage is bogging you down. It can mean that limiting beliefs and behaviors have created beliefs that are keeping you stuck and preventing you from seeing things another way.

How do these beliefs show up? They show up in almost every area of life. For example, you may see it in relationships, and it could look like this:

A previous belief that you're less than, unworthy, broken, or not enough in some way has you settling for behavior you'd never tolerate if you felt better.

A previously painful experience (like abuse, abandonment, or betrayal) has you believing that it's simply how relationships work, so you need to find a way to accept it.

A previous experience with a toxic friend, boss, or coworker has you believing there's nothing that can be done about it, so do your best to accept the toxic behavior.

Those beliefs keep you in a painful place, and the longer you stay in that spot, the worse it gets. Please know that I'm not saying to flee the minute relationships get uncomfortable; that's not what I'm saying at all. It's often the discomfort that helps us grow, and it can actually take relationships to the next level of trust and intimacy. What I **am** saying is that the belief that there's nothing you can do about it, or nothing better you can hope for, coupled with the resignation that prevents you from believing/saying/doing anything different, slowly hardens you.

"Healed," on the other hand, is to make sound or whole. To make well again, to restore, and to correct[2].

Using the examples above, here's how they'd look if you were healed versus hardened:

A (previous belief) that you're less than, unworthy, broken, or not enough in some way had you settling for behavior you'd never tolerate if you felt better. It dawns on you that you are worthy, deserving, and lovable. You start by giving yourself all the love you may never have received in the past, so you realize how wonderful you are. From that space, you can't help but radiate love, because that's who you are. Since like energy attracts like energy, you can't help but attract that same love you've been giving others right back to you.

(adultery, addiction)

A previously painful experience (like abuse, abandonment, or betrayal) had you believing that it's simply how relationships work, so you need to find a way to accept it. You've done your research; you've done the work to heal, and you realize that "even though it was done *to* you, it's not *about* you." While that time in your life was intensely painful, all you've done to move through it has created a version of you that's whole, healed, healthy, and transformed. *community*

spouse, parent(s) family

A previous experience with a toxic friend, boss, or coworker had you believing there's nothing that can be done about it, so you do your best to accept their toxic behavior. It occurs to you that this was exactly the push you needed to either speak up or start that business you've been longing to start. You find your voice, and in doing so, you subtly change the rules around how people treat you. You simply don't tolerate toxic behavior, and the more you work to grow through it, the more you realize that you've been personalizing their behavior when it actually has nothing to do with you. You see it so clearly, and instead of seeing through the eyes of anger, you're compassionate, because you realize: "Hurt people, hurt people."

It doesn't excuse the behavior; you're still not tolerating it, but you see where it's coming from, and it doesn't hurt you anymore.

Where have your experiences left you? Not sure? No worries, that's what this book is all about. See, nothing is wrong or a problem unless it's preventing you from being, doing, or having what you want.

So often, we consider ourselves healed from various types of crises such as heartbreak or devastation of some kind (i.e., abuse, neglect, financial crisis, divorce, death of a loved one, disease, a tragic accident, or betrayal). We believe we've healed because time has passed, or because those people are no longer in our lives. While removing those people from our lives can help (such as in the case of a toxic relationship), that doesn't mean that they still don't have a toxic hold on your mind and heart. And if they do, you're not healed—you're hardened.

Let's take a betrayal that happened years ago. While the betrayal is over now, there's a good chance you still might find it hard to trust. You might question your worthiness, or your confidence can be shaky. You might fear rejection, abandonment, and repeat betrayals. Struggling with these challenges? That's how you know you're not healed—you're hardened.

How about the possibility of a new business venture? If your first reaction was, "No way! I'm never doing *that* again! The last time I trusted a partner, I was totally ripped off, so I'm not even *considering* that again." I'm not saying to throw caution to the wind at all.

But, when your first response is based on an inflamed reaction to something that happened in the past, the pain and all it created is still there. That's not healed—it's hardened.

While using these painful experiences to create different outcomes can certainly help us heal, we become hardened when we:

- Neglect to look at our experiences in order to see what isn't working.

- Put that big wall up to prevent anyone from getting close to us again.

- Use things to numb, avoid, or distract ourselves from something painful to feel or face.

So how do you know where you stand, so you know what needs attention? While that's what you'll learn in this book, you can also take the **Healed or Hardened Quiz** here HealedOrHardenedQuiz. com to find out which Force of Nature you are. It takes less than two minutes, and it'll show you if you're closer to being Willow, Cactus, Bamboo, or Lotus. Got your attention? I hope so! You can find it here: HealedOrHardenedQuiz.com. I'll also explain it in a little bit, so hang in there.

Where Are You?

Here's another way to tell where you are on the healed-or-hardened spectrum:

When the pain is still there … when you're easily triggered … when you can go right back to that time, that place, that pain … there's work to be done. That's not to say the memory will erase, but the emotional charge subsides. Anger and contempt can be replaced with compassion and forgiveness. Being naïve can be replaced with being cautious. Being stubborn can be replaced with becoming more flexible. Being resistant can be replaced with becoming more willing. Feeling so much sadness can be replaced with feeling more joy. Being a victim can be replaced with becoming a victor, and trauma can be replaced with transformation.

It's not that these experiences make us weaker. It's similar to how muscles respond to a workout. They actually break down a bit with a strenuous workout, which then leads them to grow and become much stronger. Same thing happens when we heal. There's a reckoning—a facing of ourselves to see how we're showing up, how we've been acting, and what we've been tolerating. That reckoning allows us to see ourselves clearly, so we can then decide who we want to become. Stay stuck, and we become hardened. Do the work to move through it, and we become healed.

What's the problem with staying stuck? Well, for some people, there's no problem at all. Staying stuck is predictable and gives them a sense of security around where they stand. It's sort of like the saying, "The devil you know is better than the devil you don't know." It's not good, but it's familiar, and somehow, just because it's familiar, it gives us a sigh of relief, because the familiar is far less frightening than the unfamiliar. Others have no problem with staying stuck, simply because they have no idea there's anything better. In their current level of awareness, there's no indication that there's anything other than what they're currently experiencing to even hope for ... so they don't.

This reminds me of when I was growing up on Long Island in New York. I grew up with the belief that once you graduate from high school, if your budget allows, you can go to college. In my case, the option available was a state school. So, that's where I started. The next step in the belief I had was that once you graduate, if you ever want to live in New York City, now is the only time to try it. So, with that belief, I moved into NYC, and after only seven months of living with two other roommates in a one-bedroom apartment, I decided that NYC is a great place to visit, but I didn't want to live there. So, I moved back to Long Island. My belief was that once you move back to Long Island, you either find a job on Long Island, or commute to NYC. No other options existed, so take your pick as to which one was a better fit. I tried commuting and hated it, so I found lots of jobs on Long Island. The final belief in that belief system I had was that you work in NYC or Long Island, and when you're ready to retire, you move to Florida. So, it's: Long Island, then NYC, then Long Island or NYC, then Florida until your last breath.

It never even crossed my mind that there was any other option. It was completely and totally out of my awareness that any other state or country was available to me. I simply had to choose the point that I would move to the next predictable place on my journey. When the mind expands, anything is possible, and as I slowly dismantled that belief, everything changed. I'm now living a bicoastal life between New York and California—totally not what I was originally programmed to do.

So what beliefs do you currently have that may be preventing you from thinking and living differently? What rules have been put in place that need questioning and updating? Could there be something that isn't serving you that needs to be looked at with a fresh perspective? Could hauling around old programming from the past be sabotaging your future?

This is where being comfortable can be a really big trap. You may have a decent job, relationship, and level of health. You may have a stable and predictable life. You're not really happy, but you've resigned yourself to believing that what you currently think, do, and have is "fine," and since it's too hard to think about changing anything, it's ok. And it is … until it isn't.

Sure, you can strive for being "comfortable," but what do you say to that calling of your soul urging you to expand? The quiet voice trying to let you know that, if you were willing to get out of the familiar, there's a passion project, or an exciting venture or opportunity, that would light up your soul? Sure, you can ignore it, but what do you do when the voice gets louder and louder?

You may have these internal conversations with yourself, telling yourself you're too old; it's too late; there's too much to lose; it'll be too hard, and any other excuse you may be using. Whenever I get that "soul hit," I know passion, purpose, and opportunity just knocked on the door of my heart. Sure, I can ignore it, but pay attention to those subtle messages, and it's life-changing. I've experienced these soul hits so many times and have learned to take them seriously. Yes, I go through all my excuses, and these ideas have gotten me past it—so I'm sharing them with you in the hopes that they'll help you, too.

When a great idea emerges that'll disrupt my current routine, I use a few handy scenarios to get over the hump. For example, if I have a great idea, but I know it'll take a lot of time, effort, and energy, the following two scenarios often work:

The first—once I've vocalized my idea, I imagine it as a thought bubble floating above my head and slowly floating away. Then, I picture someone looking up and "seeing" my thought bubble. They realize, "Wow, that's a great idea!" and they grab it. Now, my brilliant plan is lost to someone else.

If that one doesn't work, here's the second: I picture sitting my four kids down (they're now 26, 24, 21, and 19, but when they were younger, this worked really well). I imagine sitting them all down and saying, "That great idea I talked about? Yeah, it was hard, so I'm not doing it." I see the confused look on their faces; "It's hard? That's why you gave up? Really mom, is that all you've got?" Yikes, if the first one doesn't get me, telling my kids I didn't feel like putting in the effort for something exciting or meaningful does.

I also have a few scenarios I use for when I think I'm too old—something I questioned when I went back for my PhD at 50. I remember looking up "adult athletes" and finding men and women in their 70s and above who were strong, fit, and athletic. Many started their fitness journey in their 50s. Or, I often think of Louise Hay, founder of the publishing company Hay House, whose books I've been reading for the last 15 years. Louise started Hay House at the age of 60, and millions of people have been benefiting from her work ever since.

Or, I remember when I was getting close to my PhD graduation day. A man emailed me saying, "We're in the same cohort. I'm graduating, too, and it'll be nice to see you at graduation. By the way, remind me of your name, I'm not great with names … I'm 79." Seventy-nine and getting a PhD! I couldn't wait to meet my new friend and swore that I'd never again use the "I'm too old" excuse ever again.

What have you been telling yourself that no longer serves you? If you really listened to that quiet voice, what would it whisper? And yes, while any change may take some getting used to (for you and others it may impact), is staying where you are a better choice?

Having four kids and six dogs, it's clear I've learned how to move past my internal dialogue about things being hard, because raising all of them was … well, hard! It was also incredibly rewarding, fun, and fulfilling. You may have heard: "Nothing good comes easy." I kind of believe that, with the idea that great things take work. A lean, fit body takes time as you make the decision to eat healthy meals and the time to work out. A beautiful garden needs tending. A great relationship needs communication, love, respect, compromise, and more. So yes, these things take work, but they're so worth it.

I don't agree with that saying in that I believe joy is found in the simplest of things, especially when your head is in the right place. When you're feeling ease, joy, and gratitude, a gentle breeze could feel wonderful on your face. A sunny day, a smile from a loved one, a pleasant exchange with a store clerk, seeing a butterfly … it's the simple things in which we find joy. So, for our purposes, we're going to adopt the saying the first way I explained it.:

If you want to fully heal, moving past limiting beliefs that have been preventing the joy, passion, and purpose you're looking for, it'll take some work … but it's so worth it.

Your Baseline

Here's what I invite you to do:

Take a look at the different areas of life I'm listing below. For each, write down your beliefs. Don't overthink, judge, or critique it; simply write down your current beliefs within each of the categories. When you're finished, question every single belief you wrote down. Do those beliefs still make sense to you? Are they outdated? Does your belief need to be upgraded? You'll be amazed to see how the beliefs that were instilled in you decades ago are still the beliefs that drive your behavior today. That's totally fine if they're leading you toward the health, relationships, life, and lifestyle you want. If not, it's time to change them.

What are your beliefs around:

Health? _Its downhill from here_

Body? _Same "_

Relationships? _Are hard work_

Work/career? _Should feel rewarding & fulfilling_

Money? _Is overrated_

Religion/Spirituality? _Is exhausting_

Education/Personal Development?

Family? _Doesnt have to be blood_

Lifestyle?

Self-Care? _Is important_

It's important to write out your beliefs for each of those categories. What you'll be doing here is choosing the ones that gave you the most emotional charge. Were you surprised by some of your beliefs? Do they need updating and upgrading? There are likely a few beliefs that really don't work for you anymore, and that's great! Now you see what's been holding you back. Those are the ones to take on first to slowly and steadily move you forward.

The trap: When we have a set of limiting beliefs or are coming out of a painful experience, we move through life as best we can. We don't know that there's really much we can do to take that pain away, so we either act like it's not there or find a way to get used to it.

We're not happy, but we don't know it can get better, so we look for things outside of us to help with what's happening inside. That hole that won't heal needs to be filled, calmed, squelched. So we may start by having a glass of wine or two. We may walk over to the cabinet and grab a handful of cookies. We may numb out in front of the TV. It goes away for a while … but not for long.

We wake up the next day, and it's still there. We don't have time to look into it; after all, we're busy, and it kind of feels a little self-indulgent, especially if we're so used to caring for others, or if we're just busy and don't have much free time. Sure, we will if we can find the time. But I ask you … when have you *ever* found the time? There's so much to do: the job, the kids, the responsibilities. We put ourselves on the back burner and say we'll take care of ourselves *when we can*. We may throw in a workout or a healthy meal and think that's enough, justifying to ourselves that it's what we can do, so it's enough. But that unhealed pain inside? It's still there. So we grab a few cookies or watch some TV, or if you're like me, get really busy with work. It's a total distraction. Maybe we listen to or read a self-help book. Does it help? A little. But at the root of it all, that unhappiness is still there, and we don't know what to do.

Maybe if we realize we're numbing ourselves, we try a more holistic approach and have a Reiki session, do some yoga, or something that makes us feel more connected. Is it still there? For us pro-active folks, this feel like we're action taking, and while that may be the case, is that sense of unease still lingering? Possibly.

This book is for those who have a feeling they may be in a perpetual holding pattern. Those who are stuck. For those who can't find a way onto solid ground after a traumatic experience as well as those who are tired of carrying around—and are ready to let go of—baggage. It's for those who want to be, do, and have more, but feel like they're deeply rooted and can't … as well as for those who want to move forward but don't know how.

I'll never forget a mentor who once said, "You can't steer a parked car." Are you parked? If so, we're going to find the exact key you need to get yourself in motion. Are you healed or hardened? Yes, you have every right to be hardened. No one is questioning that, but it's taking away from your joy, your freedom, your peace.

So together, we're going to get to the root of it. You're going to see exactly where you stand, so you know what to do with it.

You're here to be, do, and have so much. Yet from a more hardened place, even if you have all of the things that "should" make you happy, it'll never feel good. So, let's see what's happening, and then create a plan to heal, for real.

We're doing this together.

Right here, right now. Life is calling.

Why We Can Be Hardened

At the time of this writing, there's an unsettled feeling among us. Covid forced us to change everything about our lives. Many lost their jobs, their income, their health, and their lives. Others lost their self-esteem, sense of control, and ability to hide from themselves. With more time at home, "methods of mass distraction" were at an all-time high with more drinking and tobacco[3] and emotional eating to temporarily quell the uncertainty about our families, our finances, and our future. One study found that the psychological reactions to the COVID-19 pandemic may vary from a panic behavior or collective hysteria to pervasive feelings of hopelessness and desperation, which are associated with negative outcomes including suicidal behavior[4]. Other health measures may also be compromised by abnormally elevated anxiety[5].

Increases in arrests[6] were reported along with an increase in family violence[7] and child abuse[8]. Many struggled in their marriage and relationships, as well[9], as the stress couples faced became more than they could tolerate. The lack of space needed by some couples was eliminated as they spent more time under one roof. For some, it created much needed time together. For others, the divorce rate increased[10] as more time together became intolerable.

Fear was in the air. Some used the time to get to projects they'd been putting off, and while they remained socially distant, they stayed as close as they could using Facetime, Zoom, and drive-by visits.

Others were forced to face themselves. Every feeling they'd been running from was suddenly looking them squarely in the eyes. For some, this led to a time of deep exploration and growth. For others, it led to extreme behavior, explosive reactions, and internal chaos.

"Nothing good comes easy." As I mentioned earlier, that's a mantra I remind myself of when hit with hard times, or when I'm feeling emotional and experiencing mental chaos. That's a good time to remind ourselves of this truth. It's only when we work through the chaos that we come out the other side. You may have heard the expression, "The only way to it is through it." That's so true. Feel the chaos and numb yourself from it, and it's still there. Feel the chaos and find a way to move through it—and you find strength and confidence.

As if fear and worry don't wreak enough havoc on you mentally and emotionally, these emotions impact you physically, too. Fear and worry about your own health and the health of your loved ones, your financial situation or job, or loss of the support services you rely on leads to:

• Changes in sleep or eating patterns.

• Difficulty sleeping or concentrating.

• Worsening of chronic health problems.

• Worsening of mental health conditions.

So, when we've been through these things and figured out how to survive the experience, it's easy to be bitter and resentful that it happened. We didn't get what we wanted—we got something we didn't expect, and life just seems harder than it's supposed to be. If you had some unfinished challenges before, then adding something like Covid, a loss of income, additional stress, or poor health to your plate can easily make and keep you hardened.

Or, maybe the recent changes haven't impacted you much, but there are still some beliefs that have kept you stuck and small. Maybe you believed you weren't smart, worthy, or deserving, so you stopped striving for more. Maybe you grew up with a negative belief about money, and instead of questioning the belief, you resented those who had what you wanted. Maybe you grew up without being told how lovable and wonderful you are, so you struggle with your confidence, worthiness, or self-esteem. And maybe you wanted to express yourself through a creative outlet that brought you great joy. But instead of being met with appreciation, you could have been met with judgment, so you stropped trying.

That's what happened to me. I grew up with the belief that *if you were having fun, you weren't being responsible.* So, being responsible became the goal, because being irresponsible (aka having fun) would be received with shame, blame, guilt, and rejection. With this link being formed in my mind, having fun didn't feel safe or welcomed, because I didn't want to be seen as a slacker, lazy, or irresponsible.

Instead of pushing against it, I chose to contract and contain myself. At the time, it seemed easier to stay small, bottled up, and contained than feel the judgment or risk feeling abandoned for expressing myself or taking a different path. We all have a need to belong, and it can be scary to risk doing something that may reduce our chances of staying safe within our group. I didn't want to risk anything, so I was a chameleon ... being who I believed I was supposed to be to stay safe and belong. Over time, it just became who I was, and while internally, there was a little girl who longed to be silly, giggle, and play, on the outside, it was "game on."

When we do this for a few weeks, months, years, or even decades, it's easy to see how what was originally a thought takes on a life of its own. Before long, it becomes a habit, and then it just becomes who we are ... *until we see it clearly*. I still find myself in the role of "the responsible one," and having fun isn't something I prioritize nearly enough. As I move from hardened to healed, I'm right there with you, seeing the habits and behaviors that still need my attention and direction.

When these behaviors, these traits, and this persona becomes who we are, what can it lead to?

Something just doesn't feel right. Maybe it's a pain in the neck, shoulders, or back. Maybe it's a tightness in your jaw, a clenched fist, or constricted body. Maybe it's restless sleep, exhaustion, a digestive issue, or more.

There are so many ways our bodies are telling us that something isn't right, but with all we have on our plate, who's got the time to figure it out?

It could have been something that happened years ago. If it was something traumatic, you may have placed it deeply within the subconscious, suppressing or repressing the painful memories. But those memories and that pain need a place to go, which means that while they've been stored out of reach, they may be subtly (or not so subtly) letting you know they need attention.

While you may experience physical discomfort, it's likely it's showing up as mental and emotional discomfort, too. Because we're not sure how to manage it or even where it originated, we try to outrun these feelings however we can. Here's where we turn to food, drugs, alcohol, work, TV, keeping busy, or some other behavior to temporarily quiet these emotions. We can also use these experiences as unhealthy fuel. Here's what I mean:

The Hardened Profile

Let's say you were told that you'd never amount to anything, so you're best off forgetting any dreams of abundance. That's simply for "other people." You could have interpreted it in one of two ways. The first is to believe whoever told you that is right, and it's best to settle for whatever life brings you. You also could have used "I'll show you" fuel. "I'll show you" fuel is the intense drive to prove someone wrong—to show them who's boss and make sure you protect yourself from the pain, so it can never penetrate you. It could look like this:

The boy who was physically bullied in middle school takes steroids and compromises his health to become an incredibly muscular body builder, so no one can ever hurt him again.

The girl who was the "ugly duckling" makes herself over and now devotes all of her time, effort, energy, and income to maintain her beauty and style. This is now where she gains her sense of self-worth.

The boy who grew up in poverty is so determined to make money, he compromises his health, relationships, and integrity to do so.

The girl who always felt unloved becomes a people pleaser to get that love from others, believing that's the only way she can get the love she needs.

The boy who never felt smart enough becomes the know-it-all.

The girl who never felt worthy goes to extremes to prove her worth.

It's not necessarily the outcome that's the problem, but rather the soil it's growing on. It's like a garden. Plant your flowers in rich, healthy soil, and watch a beautiful garden grow. Plant it in unhealthy soil, and while it may grow, it won't be as healthy, beautiful, or sustainable.

The motivation behind the actions is what makes us healed or hardened. The "I'll show you" fuel may get the job done, but not without a price.

However, you can exchange it for healthy fuel, and those same scenarios you exchange it for could look something like this:

The Healed Profile

The same boy who was bullied in middle school still learns how to protect himself, while also doing the work to realize that "hurt people, hurt people." It doesn't excuse the behavior, but he knows it wasn't about him. It was their issue.

The same girl who was the ugly duckling still takes measures toward looking and feeling great, yet learns to take pride in her inner as well as outer beauty.

The same boy who grew up in poverty and was determined to never experience that again still works hard and makes a great living, yet understands that it's not worth it if he sacrifices his health, relationships, and integrity to get there. He makes peace with the idea that it may take a bit longer, but the longer route is worth it, because it's not worth losing who and what he loves most.

The same girl who always felt unloved learns that no amount of validation or acknowledgment from the outside can fill a void from within. With that, she decides to focus on loving herself first, which benefits all within her care and reach.

The same boy who never felt smart enough realizes that he's very smart in regard to what he finds interesting and important. Who cares about the rest? That's what Google is for ⊠.

The same girl who never felt worthy does the work to learn that she's worthy, lovable, and deserving, simply because she exists.

It's the same experience with different fuel behind it. This is the fuel that helps us heal.

You're Meant for More

What a hardened person says:

"Been there, done that. I don't trust anyone. It's just easier that way. I'm fine. I don't care. I don't want to deal with it. It's better this way." This kind of self-talk convinces them to stay exactly where they are. Days turn into weeks, months, years, and decades. The only things that might be changing are how you feel physically, mentally, and emotionally … and not in a good way.

"Whatever. Now it's even harder. What's the use? Forget it. Pass the chips."

What if? What if this was the first day you were willing to consider that you're meant for so much more?

Here's my perspective:

Whatever led you to believe you're less than, lacking, or undeserving in any way is over. This negative belief may be stemming from a recent experience or from something that happened decades ago. Imagine that someone said something to you 10, 20, 30, 40 or more years ago, and it's *still* impacting how you live now. Not only has this person or group of people impacted you when he/she/they had control over you back then, but you're keeping it going all throughout your adulthood. Here's the worst part …

That person may not remember or even care that they said or did those things, yet you're carrying it around not just as a painful memory, but as a legacy that impacts how you think, act, and behave.

Let's say that the belief is that you don't feel worthy. Maybe that was put in place when you were a small child, and here you are as an adult making decisions based on it. Without feeling worthy, you settle for relationships in which you're treated without the love or respect you deserve. Without feeling worthy, you settle for work that doesn't inspire you. Without feeling worthy, you put yourself last and accept the crumbs given to you, versus knowing your value and standing up for yourself and your needs.

Keeping this belief alive is not only impacting who you are and what you think; it's impacting your health, too. If you don't feel worthy, you may not prioritize your health or self-care, so it's easy to let those things go as you prioritize others instead. This one negative belief, created as a child and kept alive as an adult, is stealing your joy and will continue to do so until you change it.

Now it's up to you to unravel and delete the negative programming that's created the way you think, feel, and perform. That hardened exterior isn't who you really are. It's a mask of protection, and while you may have needed it as a child, you don't need it anymore.

The Mask

It's been on for so long, we don't even know it's there. It's how others see us; it's how we see ourselves. Without the mask, we're naked and vulnerable. Screw that, that mask is going right back on!

Is it serving you?

"It's just who I am."

Really? No, it's not. It's who you *created*.

I'll never forget being at a seminar and doing an experiential activity where we had to envision our funeral. Yes, it was brutal. We had to picture who was there and what everyone was saying about us and the life we've led.

What would they say about you?

Did enough people get to know you? Did you wear out versus rust? Did you 'squeeze the juice' out of this life you've been given? I get that these aren't everyday typical questions, and that's why they're a bit jarring. I wish you could feel my heart right now!

I believe in you more than you believe in you. I see your truth. I see the version of you that's hiding under a few layers of fear, doubt, and insecurity. I see the questioning—the back and forth of your highest self, nudging you. I see your ego jumping in to have you believe it's all nonsense. It tries to convince you that it knows best, and it knows what you need. It's trying to protect you, so it doesn't want you to listen to that voice that's trying to get your attention … that soft, subtle voice gently nudging you toward something better.

Flexible Versus Inflexible

We become and stay hardened when we're rigid and inflexible. We've made up our minds about something, and questioning those beliefs isn't an option. Too much could unravel if we decide that a belief has become outdated or doesn't serve us anymore. It would create too big of a shake-up to us and those around us, so we reason that we're best off staying exactly as we are.

When we're unable to envision anything bigger or better than we currently have, we're digging our heels into where we currently are. We then protect that place and stance. In doing so, a few things happen. We can believe that it's "our way or the highway," rendering the ideas or suggestions from others as having no value or merit. Could there be a helpful suggestion in there somewhere that may support us somehow? Possibly, but it's not worth the risk of making changes to the setup we've created.

We can have a strong need to be right and reject or even become offended by any other idea that doesn't support our current belief or what we currently agree with. Here, we only like the ideas similar to our own and don't dare consider a different or new perspective. From this rigid and inflexible place, maintaining our views and perspectives is the priority. It's more important to be right than to potentially learn something new. With our rigid stance in place, we're putting up a wall that can't be penetrated with a new viewpoint, idea, or suggestion. Those things could potentially break down our wall, and if staying behind it has become familiar and comfortable, we'll do just about anything to maintain it.

Can you see yourself taking a more rigid and inflexible stance to your growth, health, relationships, finances, and more? Now let's take a look at what a more flexible perspective can look like and how it moves you toward healing.

With a more flexible approach, we have an open mind and allow for the possibility that there's more to learn. From this place, we know that what we've done has gotten us here, and if we want to go to the next level, it's going to take a new way of thinking, acting, and behaving.

This was the exact line of thinking that put me on a spiritual path. I remember consciously saying, "Just because I don't understand it, it doesn't mean it doesn't exist, or it's not true." That one statement led me to pursue ideas in all things we can't see, like spirituality, quantum physics, the power of the mind to help us heal, and so much more. Like a kid in a candy store, this one statement has led to decades of going through my days with a curious mind. That curiosity has allowed me to learn about things that a closed mind wouldn't consider or would make excuses for. To those with a more closed mind, magical synchronicities would be considered nothing more than a coincidence. Intuitive hits and divine moments would be called "crazy," "woo woo," or "weird." To me, the unknown has so much to offer, and I've chosen to be a lifelong learner of the seen and the unseen, the known and the unknown. To those who disagree? That's ok! Bringing up those topics is my way of seeking out "my people."

There are other important aspects of being more flexible, too. When we're judgmental, we're making an assumption about something that may or may not be true. Can we really ever judge anyone if we haven't walked in their shoes? This is something I personally work on daily, and a recent incident just showed me I have more work to do.

I had an appointment scheduled with someone who was interviewing me on their podcast. Two minutes before the recording, I got an email that the recording was cancelled. Immediately after, I got a follow-up notice that it had been rescheduled for another day and time. My initial reaction? "This was so rude and unprofessional.

Such complete disrespect for my time. I planned around this and could have planned my day differently if I knew I'd have that hour free." I kept going: "Reschedule our appointment time, assuming I'd be available and happy to show up with the hope that this time, we'd get our interview done? No thanks. I'm not wasting my time again. It's ok. I'll pass on the interview." So when I found out that his wife went into labor and he was on his way to the hospital … I realized I'd judged way too quickly.

More flexible people also listen in order to understand someone versus rehearsing what they'll say the minute the other person stops talking. They know that the other person may be dropping valuable nuggets, and they're open and receptive to hearing them. They're not worried that a new perspective might try to tear down their beliefs. Instead, they're eager to learn something that they hadn't thought of before. New ideas are welcomed and can be incorporated into their current belief system. Learning something new makes them richer and more complete as a result, versus feeling threatened by outside information that may compromise what's already been created.

A Bit of Backstory

If you've read my book, *Trust Again: Overcoming Betrayal and Regaining Health, Confidence, and Happiness* thepbtinstitute. com/trustagain, then you're already familiar with **The Five Stages from Betrayal to Breakthrough**. If it's the first time you're hearing about the **Five Stages**, allow me to give you a bit of a summary. First, though, I'm going to give you a bit of the backstory.

There's a really important reason why I'm sharing the stages here. First, while they were discovered as a result of my PhD study on betrayal, they can be applied to moving through most challenging experiences. As you read them, try to see if you can find yourself in any of the stages. If you're closer to being healed, it's likely that you're in Stage Four or Stage Five. If you're a bit more resistant, inflexible, and hardened, your experiences and beliefs may be due to a painful experience that has you in Stage Two. Or, if you've figured out how to survive your experience, and that's where you stayed, it's likely you'll see yourself in Stage Three. Be careful not to judge yourself wherever you land. You were doing the best you could with what you had available to you at the time.

Years ago, I experienced a painful family betrayal. I'd grown up with verbal, emotional, and mental abuse that had me believing I was flawed and unworthy. It took years of hard work to finally believe that even though I was on the receiving end of the damaging words and behaviors, it really wasn't about me. It was their inability to take responsibility for their actions and behaviors that had me believing it must be my fault, and I spent my earliest years constantly trying to prove I was worthy, deserving, and lovable. You may have experienced this yourself where you're getting blamed for things you didn't say or do, but because the people you trust are the ones saying it, you believe there's got to be some merit there, so their belief becomes yours. That's what happened to me.

Taking a Stand

The silent treatment was one of the punishments I'd receive if I did anything "wrong" (and "wrong" often meant that I didn't take responsibility for something I didn't even do). It was also the most brutal of punishments, because it felt like emotional death. It felt like my oxygen supply was being cut off, so I'd do anything and everything to get that oxygen supply back. I'd apologize, try to make amends, and basically become a chameleon, so that I could have the character traits that would win back their acceptance. I did this for years.

I'll never forget the day I said to myself, "If the only way they'll love me is if I apologize and try to win back their love every time something happens, I don't want it anymore." I was 19 years old, and I was done living with these types of rules and with this type of conditional love.

It took two years—two solid years until anyone in my family reached out to me for anything other than absolute necessities. It was so heartbreaking to realize that their pride and ego were more important than me, but the proof was there, and it was a long and hard two years. Then, one night while I was a senior in college, there was a knock on my dorm room door. It was my mom. She didn't have to say a word. The action of finally looking for me, caring enough about me to reach out, made all the difference. I hugged her, and the relationship began to change based on a painful-yet-new respect for me that never would have happened had I not stood my ground.

From that time until she passed, we slowly healed from our rocky past. She'd gotten cancer, and I felt blessed that we had seven years to work out lots of issues. She even apologized for the first time, and it was a shock to realize that people can and do change. Unfortunately, it was under dire circumstances, but it was helpful to hear nonetheless. These few years proved to be a beautiful time together, as we both realized that the clock was ticking and there was no time to waste. I purposely had my first two children very close in age, so she'd have an opportunity to meet them—something I'm so grateful for. She used to say, "Please bring me my medicine." Her 'medicine' was my kids … her grandchildren, who she was always so thrilled to see. She only got to meet my older two, but she treasured those moments. We talked endlessly, cleared up all we could, and when I knew we were getting close to the end, I had an idea that I want to share with you. I'm so grateful I thought of it at the time, and if you're in this position, it may help you, too.

The Pillow

When it was obvious that my mom was nearing her final days, I went to a store and bought a small, decorative pillow. On it were the embroidered words, "mother and daughter." I brought it with me one day when I went to see her in the hospital, and when I pulled it out of a large Ziploc bag, I said, "Mom, see this pillow? This is a love pillow. I'm going to put it on your chest and help you move your arms so you're hugging it over your heart, ok?"

She slowly nodded her head in agreement. I put the pillow on her chest and gently moved her frail arms over it to hug it close to her heart. Then I said, "Mom, I want you to squeeze in all of the love, the hopes, the dreams, the wishes, the intentions, the ideas, the plans, the joy, and everything you can think of into this pillow. I'm going to be holding it close to my heart, too. I'm going to be looking for your guidance, and I want to be sure it's all in there. Ok?" She agreed, and I saw her close her eyes and give the pillow a slow and gentle hug. I asked, "Are you done? Is it all in there?" Her eyes were closed, and she slowly nodded to indicate she wasn't finished as I watched a tear fall down her cheek. I was crying, too, not wanting to rush this beautiful process, because I knew I'd be counting on that pillow in the days, weeks, and months to come. "Need more time, mom?" She slowly nodded "yes," so I took a deep breath and waited. A little while later, I asked again, "Is it all in there, mom?" She nodded "yes." I told her; "Thanks, mom. I love you."

I gently moved her arms aside, took the pillow from her chest, and quickly put it in the large Ziploc bag and sealed it. I didn't want any single thought or intention to escape the pillow or that bag, and somehow, quickly putting it in the bag and sealing it felt like the best way to ensure everything was exactly where it should be. A few days later, she passed. I slept with that pillow for weeks, trying to imagine every thought, intention, and idea she was trying to tell me when I needed comfort. It helped tremendously, and while I still missed her terribly, this pillow and what it symbolized helped me while I grieved her loss.

Since my mom was the "glue" that kept the family together, everything went haywire after her loss. No need to get into details, but a painful family betrayal rocked me to my core. I set out to do the necessary work to heal (by this point, I'd become familiar with people saying, doing, and behaving in ways I'd never understand). I pulled out the strategies I'd used years earlier to understand once again that "hurt people, hurt people." I somehow knew that my family would be the one I create versus the one I came from, and that's exactly why I was so intent on having a large family.

The Quest

Around that time, a deadly disease called peritonitis nearly took my life, landing me in the Intensive Care Unit of our local hospital for 11 days. While every doctor was baffled at how I managed to survive the infection that was quickly ravaging every one of my organs and systems, I'm convinced it was the fierce decision I made to survive for the sake of my family that turned things around. My insides were a mess. The surgeon said they'd suctioned out between a pint and a quart of strep pneumonia from me. I was quarantined in the ICU, and it was truly a miracle that I made it out of there alive.

So, when I had that thought that I'd better create my own family, because I soon wouldn't have the one I came from, it became a quest. Don't get me wrong; I was so grateful I had my daughter and my son, but every mom knows when she's done having children. I'd always dreamed of having close siblings—best pals to share life with—and since I didn't have that, I wanted to be sure my children did. I also wanted to be sure that, if they didn't get along with one sibling, there were others to choose from, and while there may be differences in opinion, they all had one another, especially when they got older. Well, I didn't count on the idea that the peritonitis made my insides look like a tornado went through it. There was so much damage and scar tissue, and certain body parts weren't even all there or where they should be. So to say it was challenging getting pregnant with my third child is an understatement.

I tried every fertility treatment available that our insurance covered and paid out of pocket for the rest. Month after month with no success. I was giving myself injections, taking medications, and trying everything the fertility specialists advised without any results other than reactions to the medication and frustration. I thought there must be something wrong with the approach we were taking, so I changed specialists and met with the doctor who said, "Your insides are a mess. You don't even have all of your parts. You'll never get pregnant normally. You have to bypass your tubes. Maybe then you'll have a shot with in vitro fertilization."

It was going to be a big undertaking, but I was going to give it one last shot. If I tried everything I could and it didn't work, it wasn't meant to be, and I could close the door knowing I did everything I could think of. That still would have been wonderful, because I was blessed with my two kids—but after a lifetime of family craziness, I was determined to give my kids something better than I came from, if I could.

Eager to get started, I did everything I was supposed to. I got pregnant … and miscarried. It took time to grieve the loss, but when I was ready, we tried the process one more time—one more opportunity for the process to work to create the family I longed for. At that point, the doctors told me that there had been advancements made, and it was likely the process would have me pregnant with twins. I was ecstatic. Bring it on! I was ready. The process was complete, and I was imagining buying two of everything as I welcomed twins to my growing family. I could barely contain my excitement!

A few weeks later, I crumbled on my bathroom floor and cried. The process didn't work, and my dream of a large family was over.

High hopes and expectations are often followed by a hard crash, and that's exactly what happened. I was angry, bitter, and resentful. It turned into a full-blown pity party as I added onto my "Why me?" I mourned the loss of my mom and the baby I miscarried and wondered why I had to have a crazy family that messed up my mind and self-esteem so badly AND a disease that nearly killed me and left me with a nine-inch souvenir scar. I topped it off with the added frustration of a struggling business, health issues, exhaustion, and anything else I could think of to add to my story. I was so frustrated and couldn't figure out why, if I was a good person doing everything right, it was happening to me.

I'm sure you've felt this way at some point, too. You're playing by the rules, being a good person, and WTH! You just want a break … something to go your way. You want to be thrown a bone when it feels like all you do is try without any success. That's how I felt, until

I once again pulled out my toolkit of strategies and slowly came out of the emotional prison I'd locked myself in.

It started with the wake-up "frying-pan-to-the-head" realization that I had two beautiful children, and maybe that was all I was supposed to have. I didn't shortchange my grieving process, though. I decided to cry when I needed to and looked forward to the day that memories would be comforting instead of painful. I realized that my huge scar told a powerful story of survival, and since it went down the midline of my abs, I could choose to cover it or see it as actually helping to create a defined ab look (kinda). I realized that the abuse I came from would serve as amazing lessons for what *not* to do when it came to my own family, and I made changes to my business that allowed for more people to learn about me and my work.

Making sense of the senseless isn't always easy, and that's why I believe it's helpful to trust in the unknown. Whether you call that God, The Universe, Divine Spirit, Energy, or something else, it's times like these when we're best off surrendering it up to the Universe (or whatever you believe in) and trust that everything has a reason, even if we don't understand it.

That trust, along with daily work to make sense and meaning out of my past, led to tremendous healing—physically, mentally, and emotionally. I even remember making peace with the idea that we were a great family of four, so there was no need for the bigger car. I thought about all the money we'd save without the expenses of a larger family. I sought out kind, like-minded people, proving that there are all types of people in the world, and if I could attract quality people into my life, I couldn't be *that* bad. This belief helped me heal from that old, negative programming. I even looked at my body differently, thinking, "If this body isn't going to 'work' the way I want it to, I can at least get it really healthy." With that, I created a new nutrition and fitness plan. I was eating well, exercising, and getting into shape. I felt like I'd entered into a new chapter of life, letting go of so much pain and preparing myself in the best way I could for the future.

It's amazing what can happen to the body when we turn down the stress response. I stopped dreaming about the future and felt good about the present. I stopped striving for something I couldn't have and started making peace with my past. I let go of what I had no control over and started getting excited about what was within my control. The acceptance led me away from anger and toward self-love. I'd been so hard on myself, and while I'd been through a lot, the anger, bitterness, and resentment had kept me sick and stuck.

Letting it go slowly and steadily felt like I was leaving a giant suitcase filled with pain behind me, and it felt freeing. It was around that time that I'd get really dizzy and nauseas after my workouts. I thought it was my diet, so I changed a few things. Nope, still nauseas. I couldn't imagine why, until a dear friend looked at me one day and said, "I think you're pregnant." What??!! No chance. It's a wreck inside this body, no way! "Why don't you take a pregnancy test? I just have a feeling." So, I did … and I was pregnant with my third child. (Later, I got pregnant again with my fourth.)

These were two miracle babies, fiercely determined to come into the world, because as the fertility specialists had all claimed, "Your insides are a mess. It looks like a warzone in there." I can only imagine that these two kids wanted me as their mom as much as I wanted them as my children.

Healing from the family issues would take years of work, which I was willing to do every time a trigger, reminder, or painful exchange reared its ugly head. It felt challenging, but worth it as I saw how my growth was having a positive impact on my kids and clients. I got into a steady rhythm managing my family, work, and busy life.

Then, in August of 2015, I got the call that changed my life. It was another betrayal, but this time, it was my husband.

Oh No, Not Again

Talk about crashing and burning. Everything in the past seemed like necessary preparation for what I was now facing. I tell the whole story in **Trust Again** thepbtinstitute.com/trustagain, but in short, it was devastating. I looked at the two betrayals—first by my family and now by my husband—and asked myself what was common to both experiences. I realized that boundaries would easily get crossed, I didn't take my needs into account, and I struggled with my sense of self-worth. With that, it was time to do something drastic, because as you'll hear me say so often, "If nothing changes, nothing changes."

I was desperate to understand how the mind works, why people do these things, and how I could heal. That search led me to a PhD program in Transpersonal Psychology: the psychology of transformation and human potential. While I was there, I did a study on betrayal: what holds us back, what helps us heal, and what happens to us (physically, mentally, and emotionally) when the people closest to us lie, cheat, and deceive. What happened next changed everything.

That study helped me make three groundbreaking discoveries. It became crystal clear as to exactly why people become and stay stuck. More importantly, it revealed a roadmap of what to do in order to move out of that stuck place, using your experience as a launchpad for transformation.

I'm sharing those three discoveries here, because whether you've experienced betrayal or not, I'm going to show you how easy it is to get stuck after a negative experience. This way, you can see if that's what's been stopping you, so you can slowly and steadily make changes that take you to where you want to go.

The Discoveries

1. Post Betrayal Transformation:

The first discovery was that healing from betrayal is very different than healing from other life crises, like the death of a loved one, disease, etc. I compared betrayal to the loss of my mom, being in the ICU with peritonitis, and the other challenges I'd faced, but betrayal felt completely different. I didn't want to assume that what I was feeling was the same for everyone in my study, so I asked all my study participants: "If you've been through other traumas besides betrayal, does it feel different to you?"

Some had also experienced the death of a loved one. One participant also lost all of her belongings in a fire that burned her house to the ground. Another had a loved one experience a tragic accident, and regardless of what their other traumas were, betrayal felt so different to them, too. Why? *Because it feels so intentional that we take it so personally.*

Betrayal shatters trust, a sense of belonging, worthiness, and confidence. We can feel rejected and abandoned, too. This all takes a toll on the self, which completely needs to be rebuilt in order to fully heal. So, when I discovered this, I coined a new term: Post Betrayal Transformation—the complete and total healing of yourself and your life after an experience with betrayal.

2. Post Betrayal Syndrome:

The second discovery was that there's a collection of physical, mental, and emotional symptoms so common to betrayal, it's now known as "**Post Betrayal Syndrome**." We've had tens of thousands of people take the Post Betrayal Syndrome Quiz thepbtinstitute.com/quiz to see to what extent they're struggling. Every age is represented, and people have taken the quiz in almost every country.

One thing I found so interesting is that we've all heard the saying, "Time heals all wounds." Well, I have the proof that it's not true.

There's a question on the quiz that specifically asks, "Is there anything you'd like to share?" While people share their stories, along with the physical, mental, and emotional symptoms they're experiencing, they also respond by writing things like: "My betrayal happened 35 years ago; I'm unwilling to trust again." "My betrayal happened 40 years ago; I can still feel the hate." "I was betrayed 25 years ago, and if feels like it happened yesterday." We've learned that, when it comes to betrayal, it'll follow you around like a shadow, show up in every area of life, and dampen all that's meant to be joyful, until and unless we "face it, feel it, heal it." That brings me to the final discovery, which showed just how easy it is to stay stuck and become hardened instead of healed.

3. The Five Stages from Betrayal to Breakthrough:

The third discovery was that while we can stay stuck for years, decades, and even a lifetime (and so many of us do), if we're going to fully heal (going from symptoms of Post Betrayal Syndrome to the fully healed state of Post Betrayal Transformation), we're going to go through five proven and predictable stages.

I'll never forget when my PhD program chairperson read my data and said, "Debi, I believe you discovered a process here." Why was that so exciting? Because that was the moment we knew there's now a roadmap for going from betrayal to breakthrough.

So, here's a summary of The Five Stages from Betrayal to Breakthrough. We're going to spend most of our time in Stage Three, and you'll see why. (Please refer to **Trust Again** thepbtinstitute. com/trustagain if you'd like a more in-depth look into the stages, including experiential exercises that can help you move from one stage to the next.)

Now that you know a little bit more about me and my story, take a walk through the stages. Most importantly, pay close attention to which stage most closely resonates with where you are right now.

Summary of the Five Stages from Betrayal to Breakthrough

Stage One: Disproportionately prioritizing physical and mental over our emotional and spiritual needs. Stage one is like a "set-up" stage, and I saw this with every participant (including me.).

Imagine four legs of a table: physical, mental, emotional, and spiritual. What I saw with everyone was that they were leaning heavily on the physical and mental legs, often neglecting the emotional and spiritual legs. So what does that look like? It looks like we're really good at "thinking and doing" (using our mind) and not really good at prioritizing the "feeling and being" (tuning into our heart). The feeling and being is where our intuition lies, and we often turn that down—and pay the price.

Let's go back to the table. With only two legs strengthened, it's easy to see how that table would topple over. And that's what happens to us.

Stage Two: The breakdown of the body, mind, and worldview. This is "D-Day" (Discovery Day). Here's where you receive the news that will forever change life as you've known it. It's a complete shock to the body, mind, and heart. Here's what happens:

Physically, the shock ignites the stress response, which means you're headed for just about every single stress-related symptom, illness, condition, and disease. Mentally, lots of changes happen, too. You can't wrap your mind around what you've just learned. It makes no sense. The room spins, and it's nearly impossible to process what you've just learned. Finally, your worldview is shattered. That's your mental model—the rules that keep life in order and prevent chaos. They're rules around who to trust, who's safe, and how things work, and in one earth-shattering, soul- crushing moment, they are all shattered. It's the scariest stage, because here is where the bottom truly falls out on us. There's no new bottom that we can sense yet, so it's terrifying. In this stage, we're scared, frantic, lost, confused, and desperate to feel better.

Stage Three: Survival Instincts Emerge. If the bottom were to fall out on you, what would you do? You'd do anything you could to stay alive and stay safe, and that's Stage Three. It's the most practical stage where we ask questions like: "How will I survive this?" "Where do I go?" "Who can I trust?" "How do I find solid ground again?" "What do I do now?" Then, once we figure out how to survive, here's what happens ... and here's why Stage Three is the hardest to leave:

Because survival feels so much better than the shock and trauma that we just came from, we take a big sigh of relief and think: "Whew! We're ok. Now let me figure out what to do next." The problem is, we have no idea that it gets any better than Stage Three (we don't know Stage Four and Five are available to us), so we resign ourselves to thinking: "This is as good as it's going to get, so I'd better get used to it." When that's the belief, a few things happen ...

The first is that we start getting all kinds of "small self-benefits" from being in that space, otherwise known as "secondary gain." We get to be right. We get someone to blame. We get a target for our anger. We get our story. We get sympathy from everyone we tell our story to. We also don't have to do the hard work of learning to trust again. It feels too big and too hard, so we figure, "Forget it; I'm not trusting anyone," and in some way, it helps us feel safe and protected as we slowly build a wall around our hearts. Here's what happens next:

Stay in this stage long enough, and some new ideas take form and can unfortunately take hold. We can start considering ideas like: "Maybe I deserved it." "Maybe I'm not all that great." "Maybe it's true what they said about me." These negative thoughts, repeated over time, pick up momentum. Add some feeling to it, and they become beliefs. Keep repeating them, and they become the foundation for other thoughts, actions, habits, behaviors, decisions, and more. Between your story and the beliefs you're creating, you start planting roots in this space. Here's what's next:

Like energy attracts like energy. So, because you're feeling less than, unworthy, undeserving, unlovable, and all those other negative feelings the experience created, your energy attracts exactly what you feel. Your mind always wants to prove you right, so if you believe you're unlovable, unworthy, undeserving, and more, your mind will find confirming evidence to support your belief. So now you're finding situations, circumstances, and people coming toward you to confirm that this is where you belong. Here's also when the "misery loves company" crowd shows up. So now you have your painful story, ideas that have you thinking somehow, it's about you, and confirming evidence from the people who begin to show up in your life. If you weren't stuck enough in Stage Three, this is the glue that keeps you there.

You're not happy in this stage, but you don't know that there's a Stage Four and Five waiting for you. You don't know how to make those uncomfortable feelings go away, so you start looking for ways to numb, avoid, and distract yourself from the feelings. What do you do?

Maybe you choose food, and you binge whenever these painful feelings come up. You stuff yourself to stuff the pain. I'll never forget working with a client who'd been a lifelong emotional eater. When I asked her why, this was her response: "I eat so I don't feel. I don't want to feel, because if I do, I'm going to cry. If I start crying,

I'll never stop." Food is so often used as a way to squelch that inner voice from being heard.

We can also use drugs, alcohol, work, TV, keeping busy, people-pleasing, and perfectionism. We dive into these "methods of mass distraction," and while they may keep the feelings at bay, nothing is happening to move us through our discomfort. We're simply trying to outrun it. Here's the problem …

You receive some bad news or have something traumatic happen, and the shock and trauma of the experience has you panicking. You eventually find your way back to solid ground and do all you can to survive your experience. You're surviving, and you feel that's as good as it's going to get. Uncomfortable feelings arise, and you do all you can to squelch them, so you choose one of those methods mentioned. You do that for a day, a week, a month, a year, five years, 10 years, 20 years. I can see someone at the 20-year mark and say, "Do you think your drinking (or emotional eating, or numbing out in front of the TV, etc.) has anything to do with your betrayal?" They'd say: "No chance. That happened 20 years ago!" But do you see? From the moment they figured out how to survive their experience and beyond, they've stayed in a perpetual "holding pattern." They entered Stage Three and became hardened, and that's exactly where they stayed.

We'll dive in deeper to Stage Three, but I want to show you what's waiting for you in Stages Four and Stage Five. (By the way, Stages Four and Five are where transformation begins. If you're hardened, there's a good chance you're stuck in Stage Three.)

Stage Four: Finding and adjusting to a new normal. Here's where you recognize, accept, and acknowledge that your old normal no longer exists. It's just not an option anymore. In the example of a betrayal, it would look like this: you accept that you can't undo your betrayal, but you *can* control what you do with it from here on out.

I always liken this to moving. If you've ever moved to a new house, office, apartment, etc., you've likely noticed that it didn't feel cozy right away. You didn't have all the details figured out, like your route to your favorite coffee place or how to get to the post office, but it was going to be ok. In this stage, we're not physically healing yet, but at least we've stopped causing the massive damage we were causing in Stages Two and Three. Here's where we're readjusting, starting to create new rules and boundaries for ourselves, and beginning to settle into the new space we're going to eventually call "home."

What's also interesting about Stage Four is this:

Think about it—if you were to move, you don't necessarily take everything with you. You don't take the things that don't represent who you want to be when you're in your new space. If your friends weren't there for you, or if you picked up a few friends from the "misery loves company" crowd, here's where you outgrow them.

Once we've settled in, we move to the most beautiful stage—Stage Five.

Stage Five: Healing, rebirth, and a new worldview. Here, the body starts to heal. We didn't have the bandwidth for self-love, self-care, eating well, and exercising until now. We were busy surviving, and those were some of the last things on our mind. Now, we prioritize ourselves and our self-care, or at the very least, realize we need to spend more effort and energy on ourselves. Our mind begins to heal as well. We're making new rules and boundaries based on what we see so clearly now. By this stage, we've also formed a new worldview as we look back on all we've been through and the road we've traveled and see just how far we've come. We look at things differently. Yes, we've been through an experience we never thought we'd survive, but we came out stronger. Yes, our heart has been broken into a million pieces, but we realize it wasn't about us. We heal our heart, and we're ready to love again. Yes, we remember when this experience left us wondering if we'd ever be able to get out of bed, let alone take care of our responsibilities, as we reflect on just how capable, empowered, and confident we've become. Sure, we have every right to be hardened by our experience, but we've chosen a different outcome. We're choosing to heal, and it feels great!

Why We Get Stuck in Stage Three

So, now that you know *The Five Stages from Betrayal to Breakthrough*, let's talk about why Stage Three is the hardest stage to leave and why you may be stuck there right now. Remember those four obstacles that are common to Stage Three? First, you start receiving all of those "benefits" from being there, like having your story, a target for your anger, sympathy, etc. Second, the longer you stay, the more likely it is that your mind starts confirming that you're exactly where you belong. You start questioning yourself, your confidence drops, and you question your value, worthiness, and so much more. Next, since this is how you feel, this is what you attract. You find yourself in situation after situation confirming your negative beliefs. Maybe you enter into another relationship that ends similarly to the last. In your mind, it confirms that it must be you that's the problem, and you must be wrong, not enough, or flawed in some way. Maybe opportunities just don't seem to be coming around as often as they did in the past. Maybe you're hesitant to explore anything new out of fear of being hurt or disappointed again. It seems easier and less painful to reject yourself, so others don't have a chance to reject you. Your world gets smaller and smaller as you close yourself off to love, intimacy, and trust.

Let's face it: all of this feels really bad, and you want some relief. That's why it's so common to reach for the food, drugs, alcohol, work, TV, keeping busy, or some other distraction, because you want relief from the uncomfortable feelings. Temporarily, the feelings are kept at bay, and you may reason that it at least makes things tolerable. So day after day, the chosen method of distraction is put in place, and before long, it's a habit.

Now, let's look at what these habits create. Let's take emotional eating, since it's something I'm very familiar with as an emotional eater myself for many years. Here's a typical scenario:

Something happens. It can be an experience, a thought that brings up negative feelings, or a trigger reminding you of something painful that happened in the past. It can also be that you're feeling overworked, overwhelmed, exhausted, bored, lonely, frustrated, or unfulfilled. You don't like that feeling, and you want it to go away. There's the food, and you reach for it.

Before you know it, you've eaten way more than you wanted to. You feel full, bloated, sluggish, and angry with yourself that you "swore you'd stop, but there you go again." Instead of the love and compassion you'd give to anyone else who fell off track, you berate yourself, disgusted and angry with your behavior. Over time, not only is this cycle exhausting and aggravating, but it also causes you to gain weight. So you still have the original issue or feeling, which is compounded by how you're dealing with it and the weight gain, which only makes you feel worse.

Think about how you trained yourself to deal with negative feelings … you eat. So every time you binge, you feel bad, and it's the perfect setup for another binge. It's a negative spiral that takes on a life of its own, while the reasons why you were looking for comfort in the first place are overlooked and neglected. On and on it goes without any end in sight.

Do this long enough and there are additional repercussions from the emotional eating, such as a lack of self-trust (you told yourself you wouldn't do it, but here you go again), a lack of confidence, because you don't like your behavior or how you feel, obesity, health issues, and more. You can exchange the eating for other vices, such as drugs or drinking, and see the same pattern. The original issue isn't dealt with. The method of distraction is in place, and not only are you still struggling with the unresolved issue, but now you're also dealing with the inevitable side effects from your vice of choice.

From that point, you may get support to get the weight off from the emotional eating and wonder why it's not working. You may get support to deal with the drinking, and while it's a great start, unless you get to the root issue, it's common to exchange one vice or addiction for another until we're ready to "face it, feel it, heal it" for good.

I'm assuming that's what you're here for, so let's keep going.

Mary and Joe

An example of what this would look like is in this scenario of Mary and Joe. Before we get into the scenario, here's one of the differences between them: Mary has been working hard to "face it, feel it, heal it," and while she used to be short-tempered and impatient, she's learned a different way to react that feels so much better. Joe didn't necessarily experience something traumatic, but he has an underlying sense of unworthiness. Why? It wasn't that he was bullied, abandoned, or any other of the typical reasons you might imagine someone feeling like that. It was in the meaning he gave to a particular experience when he was young.

Joe was about seven when he began practicing day and night to memorize his lines for the school play. It was a real stretch for him, because he'd never put himself out there like that. He'd practice his lines while getting ready for school in the morning and bed at night. He was nervous, but excited. Most of all, he couldn't wait to have his parents witness his performance, because he knew how proud they'd be when they saw how great of a job he did.

Joe asked his parents to sit in a certain area, so if he was scared, he'd know where to look to see them and feel more comfortable. They agreed that they were going to sit on the left side of the auditorium, close to the front of the stage. His mom drove him because his dad was running late, but Joe's mom assured him that his dad would be there.

It was time. The play started, and Joe's part wasn't coming up for a while, so while he tried to calm his nerves, he kept peeking at the area his parents agreed to sit. Joe saw his mom, but not his dad. The play began, and every time Joe looked, he saw his mom, but not his dad. Now, it was time for Joe's big debut. He was scared and slowly walked onstage. He immediately looked to the area his parents were supposed to be sitting, and with a sinking feeling, he saw his mom … and not his dad. His heart sank as his mom offered a forced smile as if to say, "I know dad isn't here, and I know you're hurt, but it's ok."

Joe felt unimportant. He thought he wasn't important enough for his dad to show up for something that meant so much to him. He didn't know that his dad was stuck in traffic due to a terrible accident that had him completely miss the play. Joe made his dad's absence mean that he didn't matter. Since this was the idea he kept fueling, he added emotion and feeling to it. Since our minds always want to prove us right, before long, Joe had "confirming evidence" to support his belief. Before long, he built up a strong case for "I don't matter." A string of painful relationships proved it; missed opportunities proved it; just about anything that didn't go his way proved it. Watch how his long-held belief that "I don't matter" and a lifetime of getting angry and reactive whenever that belief was triggered plays out in this scenario:

So now imagine Mary and Joe. They don't know each other, but they see each other every day at the local coffee shop where they grab a cup of coffee before heading into work. One day, Mary and Joe walk into the coffee shop just like every other day. Mary is wearing a nice outfit, and Joe is wearing a suit. They get their coffee and walk over to the table where they add cream and sweetener before heading back to their cars to go to work.

On this particular day, Mary and Joe have their coffee cups in their hands, ready to head out to their cars, and a man who was ordering his food barrels past them, spilling coffee all over them both. Here's how each reacts, based on the beliefs they have:

First, let's take Joe.

Joe has his coffee in hand, turns to head out to his car, and the man barrels past him, splashing coffee all over him and his nice suit. This of course triggers Joe's "I don't matter" issue that he never resolved. "Are you kidding me??!!! WTH!!" He's fuming and looks to the door to see if he sees the man who did it, so he can confront him. He doesn't see him there, so he races out to his car, furious that he now has to go back home and change before getting to the office. He's so angry. "Who does he think he is?" He has so much road rage, he cuts people off wherever he can as he thinks: "Are you serious trying to cut me off? Who do you think I am?" His "I don't matter" issue is raging.

He gets home and his wife is still there, as she hasn't left yet for work. She wants to tell him something cute their son said, but he quickly stops her: "I don't have time for this!" (*This* being something about their son. See, once that belief is formed, we easily replay it in how we treat others as well as how treat ourselves.)

He quickly changes, gets back into his car, and drives to the office, cutting people off with the same thoughts of, "You think you're better than me?" All is being fueled by the underlying "I don't matter" belief. As he's driving, he's thinking about who he'll tell his story about "the jerk who spilled coffee all over me and didn't even have the decency to apologize" to.

He gets to the office and starts telling the story. First to a few people, and since like energy attracts like energy, before long, he's got a small crowd around him. "Yeah, you think that's bad, guess what happened to me?!" "That's nothing … I'd take that in a second instead of what happened to me!" On and on it goes. Joe slowly realizes he's just become the President of the "Ain't It Awful Club," and he's got to think of something even better for the next day. Why? To feel important … like he matters.

The boss walks by. He needs a fourth for his golf outing, and while he'd wanted to ask Joe, he thought he'd be better off asking someone else because of Joe's negative energy. He asks Tom instead, and they have a great time. The boss then offers Tom an opportunity Joe had his eye on for a while. Joe hears about this, and of course, he's furious. This triggers his "I don't matter" belief and out of his mouth comes: "After all I do for this jerk, he asks Tom?! WTH!" On and on it goes. Just another example of Joe's "I don't matter" unresolved issue since age seven showing itself today.

Let's look at the same scenario, but with Mary this time. Over the years, Mary has realized that people do the best they can with what's available to them at the time. It certainly doesn't excuse the behavior, but it's one of the ways she's been able to heal from challenges and circumstances that have hurt her in the past. Just like a muscle, she knows that if she stops doing the work, she won't get the same result, so she makes sure she's reading books that inspire her, taking measures toward her own self-care, and journaling to uncover some blocks that have been preventing her from getting to the next level in her relationship and her career.

She gets her coffee and is about to head back to her car when the man barrels right past her, spilling coffee all over her nice outfit. She gasps and quickly thinks, "OMG, this stinks. Wait, what am I supposed to do? Oh yeah, take a breath before saying anything." She looks up and takes a breath. When she does, she happens to catch the eye of Mike, the owner of the shop, who waves her over to hand her some paper towels so she can wipe herself off. She's upset, but thanks Mike for the paper towels. Mike says, "I'm so sorry. I know that guy's wife has been really sick. When I handed him his order, he was on the phone, and I saw his face turn ghost-white. I heard him say, 'Oh my God, oh my God, oh no!' I hope everything is ok."

This hits Mary hard, and at that very moment, she lays down a new thought: "Life is short." She thanks Mike, says a silent prayer to the man and his wife, and drives back home to change. She's in no rush as she keeps repeating to herself that "Life is short." She gets home, looks in her, closet and chooses an outfit a bit more colorful than usual. It's not something she'd normally wear, but she's still thinking, "Life is short." She smiles, because she knows her friends at work will all comment on her outfit. On her way to the office, she realizes that she hasn't spoken to some of her other friends and family in a while, and it seems more important to check in than ever as she keeps thinking, "Life is short." She's then reconnecting with friends and family members, and it's so great to turn her commute into time to connect. She's a little uncomfortable, but she shares her feelings more than usual because the "life is short" theme is playing in her mind. Mary notices a fruit market on her drive and thinks that it would be nice to bring in a fruit basket to her team, just as a way of letting them know she cares as she keeps thinking, "Life is short." The fruit basket is a hit. Everyone thanks Mary, and as she reflects on the day, she commits to living with the understanding that "life is short," so it's important to live each day with that in mind.

See? It's the same experience for them both, but two vastly different reactions. Joe is stuck in Stage Three, which is exactly where we stay when we don't do anything to move out of that space. Mary, on the other hand, has spent the time and energy to move past old, limiting beliefs, and it shows in how she thinks, reacts, and behaves.

The Hardened Profile—What It Can Look Like

Meet Sue:

Sue may or may not be keeping her weight under control, but one thing she knows for sure is that her metabolism isn't working like it used to. She may be maintaining her weight or steadily gaining, but she can't figure out why. She's gaining weight in her belly, too—WTH? She never had a muffin top before, but it's an issue now, and she doesn't have the motivation to deal with it. Why? She's exhausted. Even if she sleeps a full night, she wakes up unrefreshed, dragging herself out of bed to begin her day. She may or may not exercise. When she does, it's great, and she's glad she did, but there are lots of days where the effort seems too great. And who's got the time for it, anyway?

She's busy. She's busy with chores, responsibilities, obligations, tasks, and more. She's doing everything for everyone, and there's just not enough time in the day to do it all. Sure, she's getting it done, but there's something that's unsettling … not quite right.

That feeling comes up, and to push it back down, she uses anything readily available—food, a glass of wine, or sometimes, she just numbs herself in front of the TV. The feeling goes away, but it always comes back up again. That's what the cookies, wine, and TV are for. They're the perfect distraction. She's running from that feeling, but it's catching up quickly. What's it trying to say? Is it warning her of something she needs to pay attention to? Maybe, but she's too busy to stop and find out. She keeps running from it but it's following her around like a shadow … an unease, a discomfort. It's been around so long, she doesn't know life without it. She outruns it for the night by taking something to help her sleep. Tomorrow is a new day, and she'll do more of the same.

Meet Mike:

He considers himself an average guy: he goes to work, comes home, eats dinner, watches TV, and looks forward to the weekend, when he has the time to watch sports with friends or catch up on things he didn't get to do during the week. He's content, but not making the income he wants to. When he thinks about doing something else to improve his odds of securing a raise or promotion within his company, he shakes his head thinking, "What's the use? It's not worth it." When his friends tell him about a book that inspired them, or a personal development course or seminar that they think he'd get a lot out of, he rolls his eyes and thinks it's a waste of time.

Maybe he works out, and that gives him a sense of accomplishment, because he can at least feel like he's doing something good for himself. He eats well for the most part, but usually goes overboard on the weekends.

It's a rut he's been living in for years. He's not happy with where he is in life, but squelches those feelings as he reminds himself that he's lucky to have a job. Whenever the thought of a new job or opportunity comes up, he reminds himself that he just doesn't have what it takes to make it happen. "It's just not worth it." Why not? The effort and his level of confidence. He just doesn't believe he's got what it takes, so he'd better be ok with where he is: stuck, resigned, and lifeless.

Where did these beliefs come from? Mike doesn't question them. They've been driving his actions for years, and it's just how it is.

These are also the people who may be jealous or resentful of those being, doing, and having more. "They make it look so easy." "I'm sure someone helped them get to where they are." "Whatever."

Why is it that some people harden themselves to opportunities, experiences, change, and love? Why do they put that big wall up around them, especially around their heart, keeping everyone at a safe distance?

Are they ensuring they'll never be hurt again?

Are they justifying a deep-seated belief that they're not lovable, worthy, or deserving?

Are they afraid of taking the chance that anyone could break their heart the way it was broken in the past?

Have they simply believed what others may have said, not realizing they can question, dismantle, and change those beliefs?

Who would YOU be if you questioned everything?

Who would you be if you decided that what others think about you is none of your business?

Who would you be if you decided that you've outgrown sleepwalking through life … if you realized that hard-shell exterior wasn't allowing anything great to penetrate?

What would life look like if you took on yourself, your old beliefs, your ego, your ways of protecting, numbing, and avoiding yourself and dove right in to discover who you truly are?

What if you discovered who you're meant to be and all of the strengths that have yet to be uncovered?

Is it scary? Of course. You're about to not only shake yourself up, but you're going to shake up the people around you.

Why? They kind of liked it when you were predictable. They liked it when they knew where they stood. That's not to say you're going to become cruel or heartless. Instead, you're going to become real.

You're going to become authentic, vulnerable, and honest with yourself and others.

"Oh no you don't; don't make me dive into those closets and see what's there," you may be thinking. Ok, that's fine. You can stop reading right here. If your way is working for you, there's absolutely no reason to change it. But what if there's more? What if there's SO much more? What if you haven't even tapped into your greatness? What if that protective shell was keeping ALL of it from you? What if you were willing to see what else may be waiting for you, if you were simply willing to move toward being "healed versus hardened?"

The choice is always yours.

Having worked with thousands of people for over 30 years, I've learned so much about human behavior. We do what we feel we have to do based on our current level of consciousness and on our beliefs.

If you have a set of beliefs combined with conditioned behaviors that created a need to "stay safe," then what? I'm sure on many levels, it was necessary. Maybe that's how you survived trauma. Maybe that's the only reason you're here today. If that's the case, I admire your strength and the skills you put in place to stay safe.

You're safe now.

The skills that created the need for that level of protection may have served you then, but you don't need that armor anymore. It's too heavy, too exhausting, and it's preventing you from the peace and freedom you deserve.

The Shield

Think of what a shield does. It's a rock-hard layer of protection, sparing you from absorbing anything negative, harmful, or unwanted coming your way. We put up that shield to protect ourselves. With the shield in place, we don't need to share our vulnerabilities, fears, or insecurities. They're all securely hidden behind the shield.

The shield can take many forms. Here are a few:

The shield can be money. If we use money for power, the money shield is preventing others from questioning our actions. Question our intention, and the money can stop—so the shield keeps it firmly in place. Don't question anything, and the money continues to flow.

The shield can be humor. I'm not talking about lightening things up when they get too heavy by using humor. I'm talking about using humor as a way to divert a conversation away from a vulnerable touch point. If I'm the class clown, for example, you can focus on how funny I am and not what I'm trying to hide behind all the jokes.

The shield can be perfectionism. If someone goes above and beyond, doing everything they can to be everything to everyone, you can talk about their efforts versus hitting on their potential insecurity that they believe they're not enough if they didn't exhaust themselves to prove it. Think about it: If someone believes they're enough, do you think they'd go to exhaustive lengths, flatlining their adrenal glands and making themselves sick to prove it? I'm not talking about feeling great about helping others because it's what you love to do. I'm talking about going to endless lengths because it's what you *feel* you need to do in order to receive love, a sense of value, or whatever it is you're striving for.

Once the shield is firmly in place, we can wear it like a second skin. We've used it so many times, we don't have to remind ourselves to use it anymore. It's there, like a mask we've put on and left on. Over time, we don't even realize it's there. We've worn it so long, we don't even feel it. What's even worse is, the longer we've worn it, the more normal it seems. What's the problem with that? It becomes so familiar, we can't even imagine life without it.

The Choice—What Healed and Hardened Look Like

So on a resistance scale, where are you? Are you like Sue or Mike? Using the example from the coffee shop earlier, are you more like Joe or more like Mary?

Using my story as an example, staying in Stage Three would have been easy. All it would have taken was keeping the old stories alive—those of pain, lack, and hardship. The stories of trauma, how I'd been wronged, lied to, betrayed, and taken for granted. The stories of "why me" and all that goes with it. Add to it surrounding myself with others who are in the same mental space. Misery loves company, so rehashing my story with others doing the same would have only strengthened my story and the pain that went with it.

While we need to do this for a while as we make sense out of our experiences, it's when we stay in that spot that it becomes a problem. I have a powerful story, and I'm sure I'd get sympathy from anyone I tell it to. But, at the end of the day, that's all you get—your story. That's why it's a slippery slope, and that's why we actually get comfortable in this dark and painful space. It's a trap, because you have every right to hold onto your story. That person or those people did you wrong. They hurt you. They said or did things that were hurtful, harmful, and/or hateful. Even unforgivable.

Here's where I invite you to consider a new way to think about your experiences.

Do you know that some of the most loving, kind, compassionate, and empathetic people on the planet have often been through the worst scenarios in life? It's not that life has been easy; it's the meaning they've given their experiences that has made all the difference. It's what they've done with what's happened to them that's either kept them stuck or propelled them forward. It's how they've chosen to use their experiences that have made them hardened or healed.

The Bride

I remember a tale about a bride who was jilted on her wedding day. After planning a beautiful day and dreaming about a wonderful future with her fiancé, the day finally came … and he didn't show up.

Of course, everyone there did their best to console her. After all, they'd witnessed her dream of being married happily ever after crumble right before their eyes. Of course she was devastated, heartbroken, and distraught. If you were to check in with that woman five, 10, 15, even 20 years later, here are a few scenarios you might find:

The Hardened Woman:

She still has her wedding gown, showing it to and sharing her story with anyone who'll listen. She's been jilted at the altar, and it was devastating, embarrassing, humiliating, and expensive (he left her with the bill, too).

Her friends had been there for her for as long as they could. They kept trying to be good listeners, understand how awful it was, and always make suggestions so she could eventually put it behind her and move on. She wasn't having it, and if they weren't going to be there for her in her time of need, they were just bad friends. Who needs them, anyway?

With these thoughts continuing to poison her mind, they eventually can't help but impact her body. After all, stress creates symptoms, illness, conditions, and disease. The continual flooding of stress-induced hormones and chemicals can't help but impact our health. One of the most common ways? Gut issues, exhaustion, brain fog, and weight gain.

Now, when she speaks to her friends, not only does her experience come up in every conversation, but she's exhausted and doesn't feel or look well. She knows it, and it compounds her misery. She blames it all on him, the jilter. If he didn't do that, everything would have been perfect, in her mind. Life would have been the way it was supposed to … the way she planned. And this? This wasn't what she planned.

Her friends are eventually losing patience. They don't have lots of free time, and when they do, they want to spend it with someone who doesn't pull them down. They're doing their best managing their own lives, but they notice it's taking them longer and longer to shake off the aftereffect of their time with their friend. They eventually stop calling.

Now, in addition to being jilted and dealing with a few physical symptoms, she's angry at her friends, too. How does she interpret it? NO ONE is ever, has ever, or will ever be there for her. Her so-called friends are just another example of why people can't be trusted. She's alone, and she'd better get used to it. Don't count on anyone, and you'll be better off, because the minute you trust someone, the minute you let your guard down, the minute you're not at the top of your game, your friends want nothing to do with you. "If I'm not giving to them, they have no use for me. Screw them. Who needs them, anyway?"

She justifies another loss, proving herself right that people will leave her, and she can now add these friends to the "people who've done her wrong" list. Yep, she just proved it once again, and her case is strong.

Now let's take the same scenario with someone who took a different route—the route to being healed—instead.

The Healed Woman:

It's the most perfect day for a wedding. Our bride looks beautiful. Friends and family have all come together to share in this special day. Everything is perfect: the weather, the flowers, the venue. It's a dream come true.

She's ready, and she's nervous, because the guests have arrived, and the ceremony is about to start. Where is her fiancé? Oh, he's probably with his best man who's calming him down because he's got a few jitters. Nothing to worry about. Nothing can dampen this beautiful day. The best man finds our bride in the bridal suite where she is getting ready. He can't even speak; he can't find the words. "What?" "What's the matter?" "Are you ok?" He breaks the news that his friend just couldn't do it and can't face her or anyone.

It's not happening, and it's over.

She falls to the floor; the room is spinning. What's happening? Her closest family members hold her while they ask one of the bridesmaids to let everyone in attendance know that it's not happening. The wedding is off, and the bride is with her family. The family is so sorry, and they'll be in touch with everyone soon.

She takes a while to make sense out of it, going over every detail she can think of to see where something went wrong. What did she do? What did she say? Why wasn't she enough? She blames herself at first. Those painful feelings take her down a painful path. She wrestles with them, taking them on one by one every time they arise. She notices one day a thought that's new to her: "What if it's not me? What if it's him?"

That's weird ... where did that come from?

She's been sharing her experience with a few people closest to her. They're loving and supportive. They're not offering any answers, because there really aren't any. She shares what happened. That momentary thought, "What if it wasn't about me," comes up again. She cries, because this is a new and scary thought.

She thinks about it again and again: "What if it wasn't about me? What if it's about him?" Those thoughts are building momentum. Nothing earth-shattering just yet, but enough that she's noticing some room in her mind to consider anything other than her experience and the pain she felt. It grows, and she considers: "What would happen if I feed that thought?"

She decides to feed her mind thoughts that will help her feel better.

There's no roadmap she knows of, so she tries a few ideas she's heard of. Maybe she talks it out with a therapist, gets a few strategies from a coach, or delves into holistic practices like energy healing where she tries EFT, Reiki, meditation, mindfulness, and yoga. She tries journaling and spending time with her friends. Some practices helped, and others weren't a fit, so she keeps trying to find the right "recipe" to help her feel better.

She knows that her eating hasn't been great and starts there. She notices more clarity and less brain fog and feels a sense of accomplishment and control now that she's taken back the reins on her eating.

Since she's feeling better, she starts moving a bit more. Nothing crazy, but the movement seems to clear her mind. It feels good, and it's becoming a habit she likes.

While she's moving, she reasons that it's a good time to put some positive ideas in her mind, so she starts listening to audio books, podcasts, and music that helps her create a sense of peace, clarity, and calm.

It's working.

Now she's eating better, moving, and putting healthy ideas in her mind and body. She's feeling lighter, leaner, freer. Nothing crazy, but it's a great start.

She continues, because she's feeling the effects through the changes she's making. A friend asks, "What are you doing? You look great!" She starts talking about what she's doing, and her friends want to join her because they're seeing it work for her and they want to feel better, too. Onward and upward she goes. Do thoughts about what happened still come up? Yes, but the sadness turned to anger, then pity, and now, compassion:

"How lame that he didn't even have the guts to tell me himself and had his best man do his dirty work." "How sad that after all that time, he's too cowardly to apologize … to admit how wrong that was." "Wow, if that's who he is, I'm so glad it happened back then. If that's who he was before marriage, how would he have been with more commitments and responsibilities?" "I feel bad about my family and friends coming into town, buying gifts, and more. I know … I'm going to plan another party, just to celebrate life! No gifts! If that feels too big, I'm going to make plans with, or at least call, everyone who showed up. I'm going to tell them how much I appreciated their effort, catch up, and begin again."

She smiles as the thought warms her heart.

She's healing.

As we leave PART ONE, I hope you see the areas that need your attention. It was my intention to "till the soil"—to shake things up so that you know the areas of life you've been numbing, avoiding, or distracting. Doing so is taking up so much of your valuable energy, and since the only way to it is through it, that's what we're going to do, together.

Nothing changes without awareness. It's my hope that you're very aware of what you may have been distracting yourself from. It's those things we "push under the rug" or "hide in the closet" that don't go away. It's those uncomfortable and unresolved issues we suppress that stay right below the surface, yet reveal themselves when we're questioned, challenged, or insecure. It's the false beliefs you've convinced yourself are facts that can now be looked at, dismantled, and set free. Just as old and outdated clothes that no longer look or feel good on you need to be given away, it's the same thing with our thoughts, behaviors, and actions. These beliefs and behaviors have been formed because of our experiences, and left unchecked, they can create havoc. It's time for some spring cleaning.

Does cleaning out your closet ever really feel good? I'm not sure. But there's that sense of satisfaction, empowerment, and accomplishment that feels good after you do it. Same thing here.

Now that we know what isn't working, meet me in PART TWO, so we can take the next steps to cleaning it up as you move away from being hardened and more toward healed.

Where Do You Land?

Now that you know the stages, it's time to see where you land. I've given each stage (Stages Two, Three, Four, and Five) their own tree, plant, or flower, which perfectly represents symptoms and characteristics you have when you're in that particular stage. Are you the Willow Tree, Cactus, Bamboo, or Lotus? See which more closely resembles where you are right now.

Stage Two: The Willow Tree

Willow: Known to be beautiful, flexible, and adaptable. One of the few trees capable of bending in outrageous positions without snapping.

How we're similar: We're similar to the willow in how we go to extensive lengths to adjust, bend, and be flexible in order to accommodate others often at our own expense. This also serves as a message that the more rigid and inflexible we are, the more likely we'll break, whereas the more flexible we are, the more likely we'll adapt to experiences that come our way.

Willow: The beautiful willow tree offers shade and comfort. It's also notorious for having a short life and getting diseases, and it's also a symbol of grief. These magnificent trees put so much energy into their growth that there's little left for their own defense mechanisms. Because of that, it's common that they get sick.

How we're similar: Like so many of us, we're busy raising our families, working, taking care of others, and giving so much of ourselves to others that we're neglecting our own self-care. With little attention on protecting ourselves, and instead being vulnerable and trusting (because we had no reason not to be), we're blindsided by something we didn't expect. This experience impacts us physically, mentally, and emotionally. It's a shock to the body, mind, and spirit, because at this moment in time, we don't currently have the resources or tools to help us navigate something we didn't see coming. There's often a death to the life we've known before we find our way to rebirth the new.

Willow: The willow is also a symbol of fertility and new life. A willow branch can be planted in the ground, and from it, a new tree will grow in its place. Its ability to grow and survive is powerfully symbolic and shows how we can thrive even in challenging conditions.

How we're similar: We're stronger than we think. Traumas and life crises give us opportunities to show us who we are and who we're ready to become. Even though it may seem hard to see after a crisis that shakes up your life as you've known it, there's so much potential, along with a new life, waiting to be birthed from the experience.

Stage Three: The Cactus

Cactus: Cacti require sporadic watering. They also adapt easily to high temperatures and intense sun without suffering burns. Many of them even need direct sun to flourish. Cacti also adapt without a problem to all types of soil and can grow almost anywhere. They're also inexpensive and easy to maintain.

How we're similar: So many of us are low-maintenance. We don't ask for much and don't expect much in return. While we thrive in certain environments, we're pretty adaptable to wherever we are. While it's true we may be adaptable, is it because it's what we want? Or because we don't believe we have a right or deserve something other than what we currently have? Are we low-maintenance because it's what we want, or because it's easier than wanting something we don't believe we can be or have?

Cactus: Cacti can irritate the skin and cause other issues. While cactus flowers are very pretty, they don't always appear easily. Cactus spines do not contain any poison that can kill you, but the thorns are painful and can cause infections.

How we're similar: Once we've been through a few negative experiences or have grown up with limiting beliefs, it's easy to be hardened and prickly on the outside. Maybe it's our way of protecting ourselves, maintaining a safe distance and ensuring that no one gets too close. Maybe it's easier to reject others, so they don't have a chance to reject us. Or, maybe a shield of protection ensures that no one discovers our hurt or vulnerable sides.

Cactus: According to Chinese Feng Shui, cactus symbolizes wise spending. It is believed that cacti can redirect the negative energy and balance the house energy flow, bringing positive changes into our environment.

How we're similar: Maybe you're practical in your approach. Here, slow and steady wins the race as a more balanced approach keeps you safe and protected.

Cactus: Can help manage cholesterol, ease hangovers, control blood sugar, and even boost the immune system. Who knew?

How we're similar: How many helpful and wonderful qualities do you have hiding under a protective exterior? When we're portraying an outwardly hardened persona, it's hard for others to know how kindhearted, compassionate, empathetic, and generous we really are. What wonderful qualities are you keeping others from knowing, because they're being hidden behind a more hardened exterior?

Stage Four: Bamboo

Bamboo: Bamboo doesn't break through the ground for five years. After five years, once it breaks through the ground, it will grow 90 feet tall in five weeks. Bamboo is the fastest growing plant on this planet. It has been recorded growing at an amazing 47.6 inches in a 24-hour period.

How we're similar: We may take time to get ourselves together after a crisis. We're processing, deciding who we want to become and how we want to define ourselves after a painful experience.

Our healing process may take a while as we determine what's best for us as we pull ourselves out of a dark period. Other flowers and plants are popping up all around us and looking beautiful. As the bamboo is to other flowers—if we look at others, they seem to have it all together, while we struggle often in solitude and in silence. The healing process can feel like it's taking forever while everyone else seems to be doing just fine. We can't see the results of our efforts. It can be incredibly frustrating.

However, once we've made the decision to move forward from our painful experiences, or let go of limiting beliefs, it's like a launchpad to our transformation. We take off, and as we do, new insights, opportunities, relationships, and so much more are available to us because of how quickly we're growing and changing.

Bamboo: Bamboo is a crucial element in the balance of oxygen and carbon dioxide in the atmosphere. A grove of bamboo release 35% more oxygen than an equivalent bunch of trees.

How we're similar: Like a breath of fresh air, once we see things from a new perspective, we think, act, and react from a more positive place. Our hearts are opening again, and we're releasing the anger, bitterness, resentment, and pain. Others feel better around us as we radiate a more positive energy to all those within our care and reach.

Bamboo: Bamboo (the new shoots) can be eaten, made into fiber for clothes, used in concrete reinforcement, provide great livestock feed, and machined into numerous forms of lumber, etc.

How we're similar: As we heal and/or let go of old, limiting beliefs, we're eager and excited to reveal new aspects of ourselves that may have previously been hidden. We're more willing to explore our creativity or a new direction, revealing how versatile and interesting we really are.

Bamboo: Bamboo can tolerate extreme conditions that most plants can't survive.

How we're similar: If we've been through a challenging time, we've tolerating extreme conditions. They were hard, but we've survived, and they only made us stronger.

Bamboo: Bamboo is a symbol of strength, flexibility, and health. Its strength has been compared to steel and concrete, and it stands powerfully upright on its own, even though it's a thin reed.

How we're similar: When we move through our experience, we're proud of ourselves and feel a sense of empowerment. We're able to stand tall, all on our own, because of the strength we've gained through our growth.

Bamboo: The interconnected root system bamboo has enhances its strength. As bamboo grows, it intertwines with the dirt and roots around it, which helps it spread underneath the soil. This underground expansion helps to keep the soil together while offering additional strength to the bamboo and ensuring it doesn't get uprooted in a storm.

How we're similar: We're all connected. The strength we get from others helps us grow and become well-balanced and strong. Because of support that helped us grow strong, we're also now able to offer support to others.

Stage Five: The Lotus

Lotus: The lotus flower is seen as a symbol of purity, strength, power, fertility, new beginnings, enlightenment, self-regeneration, and rebirth. Its characteristics are like the human condition. Even when its roots are in the dirtiest waters, the lotus produces the most beautiful flower. The lotus flower grows in the deep mud, far away from the sun, yet directs itself toward it. This beautiful flower needs the mud to grow.

How we're similar: Just like the lotus that grows in the mud, our dark pasts, limiting beliefs, and painful experiences can all serve as perfect "mud" for us to blossom, producing a beautiful result. Our "mud" doesn't hold us back; it actually helps us grow as we rise above and overcome our obstacles, blossoming slowly and consistently. Just as the lotus eventually faces the sun, we move toward light and love as we shed the pain of our pasts. Just as the lotus can't grow without the mud, our pain gives us the perspective to experience great joy. We need one to experience the other.

Lotus: The lotus emerges from the water in the morning, following the movement of the sun. At night, it then closes back up and returns into the water, only to repeat the process and cycle the next day. It's as if it dies and is reborn each day.

How we're similar: After our experiences, we have an opportunity to let go of any and all outdated beliefs and habits that no longer serve us. As we do, we're letting go of the old in order to welcome in the new. During this process, we're also heightening our levels of consciousness, becoming wiser and more enlightened as we grow. It's the death of the old versions of us in order to birth the new.

Lotus: The lotus detaches itself from the water and mud, yet still remains grounded, proud, and unaffected by its surroundings.

How we're similar: As we detach ourselves from things that don't support who we're becoming, we have the energy to focus on our happiness, growth, development, and enlightenment. We become less concerned with the needs of the ego as we become more open to wisdom of our soul.

Lotus: The lotus represents purity and cleanliness, as it's able to emerge from the murky waters pure and clean. Even though it needs the mud to grow, it's unaffected by it. It's more beautiful than its surroundings; it's actually more beautiful *because* of where it comes from.

How we're similar: While we've been through trials and tribulations, our soul is always clean and pure. Regardless of our actions or the actions of others, our souls stand by, patiently waiting to offer support and direction. Our changes are beautiful because of all we've learned and how we've grown along the way.

Lotus: The lotus flower blooms slowly, one petal at a time.

How we're similar: As we commit to our growth and development, change happens slowly and gradually over time. This progress continually moves us toward becoming our next and best versions of ourselves.

If you haven't taken the **Healed or Hardened Quiz** HealedOrHardenedQuiz.com, I really encourage it. It'll only take a few minutes, and it's going to show you what stage you're in. Are you a Willow, Cactus, Bamboo, or Lotus? Are you in Stage Two, Three, Four, or Five? You'll see exactly why your current state most resembles one of these magnificent contributions of nature and learn just what do to if you're ready for more.

What feelings and emotions need your attention? Have you been numbing, avoiding, and distracting? If so, what have those behaviors prevented you from seeing or moving through? We'll be working on these things and more in PART TWO.

I'll meet you there.

PART TWO
Feel It

The Butterfly

A man found a cocoon of a butterfly.

One day, a small opening appeared. He sat and watched the butterfly for several hours as it struggled to force its body through that little hole.

Until it suddenly stopped making any progress and looked like it was stuck.

So, the man decided to help the butterfly. He took a pair of scissors and snipped off the remaining bit of the cocoon. The butterfly then emerged easily, although it had a swollen body and small, shriveled wings.

The man didn't think anything of it and sat there waiting for the wings to enlarge to support the butterfly. But that didn't happen. The butterfly spent the rest of its life unable to fly, crawling around with tiny wings and a swollen body.

Despite the kind heart of the man, he didn't understand that the restricting cocoon and the struggle needed by the butterfly to get itself through the small opening were nature's way of forcing fluid from the body of the butterfly into its wings. It's necessary in order to prepare itself for flying once it's out of the cocoon.

The moral of the story: Our struggles in life develop our strengths. Without struggles, we don't grow or get stronger. While others may want to help, transformation is a very personal process where each step is moving us closer to becoming the magnificent butterfly.

So now that you have a good understanding of what healed or hardened looks like, it's time to take a look at where you land. And here's something else worth mentioning: Once you do the work, you're going to likely get "opportunities" to see if those same old beliefs and triggers still hold their charge. I have about a million examples I can choose from, but since thinking about this one just made me laugh, I'm going to share it:

"Opportunities" Showing Us Where We Are

I'd been working to heal all my old beliefs that had me believing I wasn't worthy, didn't matter, wasn't lovable, etc. I thought I was doing great. I was managing my family and career. I was creating products and services that I was sure people wanted, and I was on a mission to get my message out to those who needed to hear it.

I created an information product, which was a CD set with a matching binder of handouts, charts, tables, and more. That product contained just about every life lesson I knew at the time. I recorded the product, created the CDs and transcripts of each lesson, got a graphic designer to come up with the perfect cover, and had a great looking binder and CD set I was selling. Anyone would benefit from this information, and I was so excited to get it out to the public. I started speaking, and spoke at an event where the event planner wanted me to "sell from the stage"—meaning, I was supposed to sell a product during my talk, and the event planner and I would split a percentage of revenue generated from each sale. This was going to be great! The product cost $497, and it only cost me about $30 to create each one. This was going to be a great day. It was a small audience, but I only needed to get this product into a handful of people's hands. If I sold even a few, it would justify the expense of traveling to the speaking event, and the meeting planner would know they made a great choice by asking me to speak to their audience.

I couldn't wait, and when it was my turn to speak, my nerves turned to excitement as I truly believed *this* product was the answer attendees were searching for. I spoke and took all the time that was necessary to carefully explain all that the product contained, the value it would give them, the transformation it would provide, and how great they'd feel walking out with a binder and CD set filled with my life's lessons.

I finished my talk, walked to the table in the back where I carefully displayed my product, and expected a "table rush," which is when there's a mad dash to the table to pay for the product or service that was just talked about during a talk. No table rush. "That's ok," I reasoned. "They're just going to slowly come over to my table when they're ready."

Nope. No one was walking over, and it felt horrible. I'm going back and forth between those two states of: "It's ok, no worries," and "OMG, this is humiliating. I suck. My talk sucked. My product sucks, and I should never have left the house."

Sweet relief! A nice woman walks over to my table to purchase my product. I was SO relieved! At least *one* person here thought my talk, information, and product was worthy of walking to the back of the room to find out more. It wasn't going to be big money-making day, but at least I could justify it somehow. If I sold at least one of my $497 products, I could reason that my information was valuable to at least one person.

Then it happened.

She handed me a $5 bill … and was waiting for her three cents change! What?! Yep. She thought my life's work was $4.97, not $497. I stared at her in confusion. It took a moment to realize that, while I valued my product at way more than $497, it was only worth $4.97 to her.

"Um, it's $497, not $4.97," I said with a mixture of feeling awkward, angry, surprised, hurt, deflated, discouraged, and disheartened all at the same time. "Oh, I'm, so sorry," she said. "I, um, I thought …" I got the message, and it was another important test letting me know that there was still work to do around feeling worthy.

When we don't feel good enough as we are, that's when it gets tricky. We may go to extremes to prove our worth through what we do and what we accumulate. We believe that if we achieve enough, it'll prove we're worthy. If we have the top-of-line cars, clothes, jewelry, etc., it'll make up for what we feel is lacking inside. Here's where we overcompensate, because we fear that being ourselves won't make the cut.

The B+ Story

Not being good enough to make the cut. That was exactly how I felt all through my earlier years. I didn't feel worthy, good enough, pretty, lovable, etc. I got my clothes from the local thrift shop or my neighbor, who gave me her hand-me-downs. My style was whatever my neighbor outgrew, and as a teenage girl feeling awkward and uncomfortable, I didn't know what to do or where to turn to feel more confident and self-assured. I did all I could to overcompensate, because I didn't believe that being myself would have been good enough.

At age 16, a friend and I were invited to go to a college fraternity Halloween party. A few things about this: first, it was just about the coolest party we could have ever been invited to. But, since we were still in high school and weren't in college yet, we were going to have to come up with a "story" about why we were there. Also, it was an Ivy League school. So now, on top of the story of why we were there, we were going to have to act smart enough to justify being there in the first place.

My friend's brother drove us to the party. He was going to the party, too, to meet up with some friends and felt like if he were there, he could keep an eye on us. He was staying in a friend's dorm on campus who had friends who were girls and lived down the hall. He arranged it with his friend that after the party, he was going to bring us back to the dorm. He was going to stay in his friend's room, we'd stay in the girls' room. We 'd wake up the next morning and drive home.

On the drive to the school, my friend and I were trying to come up with a story that would make sense. "People are going to ask what we're doing there. What should we say?" We decided to say that we were scoping out schools we might go to, and this was one of the schools on our list. "It's an Ivy League school. We're not that smart. They'll never believe us!"

"Just act smart, and we'll figure it out."

We really weren't the sharpest tools in the shed back then. Not only had we not taken the SATs that we'd be taking the following year, but we also didn't know much about the test at all. It just wasn't a part of our conversations. So imagine how I felt when this happened next ...

My friend's brother takes us to the party, and all the make-up we had on made us look older than we were. We were dancing and having a great time. A cute fraternity brother asked me to dance. "Ok, here we go. Remember my story," I thought. We started talking loudly over the music, and sure enough, the question came:

"I've never seen you on campus. Do you go here?" I said, "Um, no, my friend and I are thinking about coming here, so we're checking things out." "That's great," he said. "Hope your grades are good; it's hard to get in." I responded, "Yeah, my grades are ok." "Really? That's good. Maybe I'll see you around campus." (Now came the defining moment.) "What did you get on your SATs?" He asked casually, trying to keep the conversation going. My mind was racing to come up with the perfect answer. Oh, no! I wanted to appear smart, but not too smart. Smart enough to belong, but not too smart, in case he planned on asking any more questions. I thought carefully, came up with what I thought was the perfect response, and finally responded:

I got a B+.

Yep. I said, "I got a B+" on a test that, back in the day, had a scoring system of 0-1,600. There was no B+ anywhere to be found on any part of that exam. When he laughed, I thought that maybe we had our scores in common—maybe that's what he got, too. Nope, it was just one of those moments that I look back on, cringe, and realize I would have been better off being myself. I would have been better off telling my friend that instead of acting like people we're not, going to a party we don't belong at, let's just hang out where we belong and grab some pizza instead.

Whether we're triggered, overcompensating, trying to be someone other than ourselves, ignoring our soul's calling, or distancing ourselves from our values and priorities, it's a call to look within. Think about it. If we're triggered, it's because it's something that's still not healed. If we don't feel settled, it's because we're being called to look at something that needs our attention. If we're creating a persona so others believe we're someone we're not, it's an opportunity to discover what it is we're so desperately trying to prevent others from seeing.

On the other hand, if we can laugh it off, not feel the emotional pain, or quickly move through our painful experiences, job well done. While I can laugh at these stories now, it's moments like that one that show us just as much about ourselves as they do about others.

Why Does My Body Hurt?

I thought I was healed, but realized I was hardened. For me, it doesn't always show up in the decisions I'm making, in how I'm reacting, or in how I'm responding. It shows up in body pain ... all over. I'm sharing this because it's likely that it may be the case for you, too.

I'd already had the Epstein Barr virus, tendonitis, bursitis, Hashimoto's, thyroiditis, fibromyalgia, adrenal fatigue, chronic fatigue, peritonitis, and rheumatoid arthritis so bad that I eventually had surgery in both feet. Adding to the list, I also have degenerative disc disease in my neck and upper back. X-rays showed that six out of seven of my cervical discs are pressing on nerves, and while I do all I can to manage it, sometimes the pain becomes so draining and debilitating that it's hard to focus on anything at all. Why am I sharing this when I hate complaining?

Our bodies are great measures of how we're doing. Think about it. A weight issue can easily show us how we may be neglecting our emotional needs by emotionally eating. Bags under our eyes can show us how we're not prioritizing our sleep. Dry skin can show us how we might be dehydrated. So when there's barely a body part left that doesn't hurt, and I haven't been training for an intense athletic event, what can that mean?

By the time something manifests physically, there's a lot that's been happening mentally and emotionally. When it's effectively handled, we feel lighter, freer, healthier, happier. On the other hand, when we're riddled in pain for no apparent reason, there *is* a reason. It's often because there's been so much negative energy and emotions that have gotten so stuck within us, the energy doesn't know where to go. You may have heard, "The issues are in the tissues," and it's so true. We may think we're doing great, but our bodies scream the truth.

On an energetic level, here's how two of my greatest sources of physical pain showed me what needs my attention. Be on the lookout when I describe this to see if you can relate.

Feet First

First, my feet. Energetically, issues with feet represent our ability to move forward, life direction, moving too slow or fast, and our ability to balance all that life hands us. Now, since my foot issues have to do with arthritis, let's add in what arthritis is tied to, which is anger, resentment, fear, lack of support, and more.

Before I understood how perfectly the body tries to show us what's going on mentally and emotionally, I looked at it from a purely physical place. I could barely walk and believed that the only solution was to find a medication or surgery to fix the issue and reduce my pain. I've shared this story in **Trust Again** thepbtinstitute.com/trustagain, so you may know it, but it bears repeating.

I went to countless doctors who told me that my pain was due to years of running that wore away the cartilage in my toes. The inflammation and pain made walking unbearable. While it didn't make sense that others could run well into their 70s while I could barely walk in my 40s, I assumed that each doctor knew better than I did. So with that, I had cortisone shots in my feet every three months for a few years.

Because I couldn't bend my big toes, it was easier to walk on the outsides of my feet, and that threw off my hips, giving me back problems, too. That was now an additional issue to treat, so I took anti-inflammatory medications, pain patches, heating pads, and whatever else could potentially offer some relief.

When the cortisone no longer worked and my back was always in pain, I opted for the foot surgery. I couldn't have surgery on both feet at a time—I figured if I had at least one foot available, I could still hop around on crutches, which would mean I could still work and take care of the kids. So, I had surgery on the foot that seemed worse followed by six weeks of wearing a cast and using crutches to get around. While it was uncomfortable, I was excited to be relieved of the pain and couldn't wait to eventually wear heels again (judge if you'd like; I wasn't ready to only wear "sensible" shoes).

The cast came off and physical therapy began ... and there wasn't much of a difference. Discouraged, I went back to my busy life and hoped it would get better over time. A few years later, I had surgery on the other foot. This time, I chose a different surgeon who promised that this surgery would work thanks to a different approach and protocol. Again, I assumed the doctor knew better than me and agreed to have surgery again.

While it was a bit of a different surgery, I still needed a cast (a soft cast this time) and crutches for six weeks. I reasoned with myself: "Well, at least this time it's the other foot, and I can still drive." "This surgeon had a better plan, so I'm sure this will work." "Can't wait to finally get all of these foot issues over with!"

After another six weeks, I didn't need the cast and crutches anymore. I was so excited to put it behind me ... to not have pain and finally feel better.

It didn't work.

Another wasted surgery, leaving me with the same pain I had before. Only now, I had scars on each food as souvenirs of the experience.

I was really angry. WTH! I just put myself through two surgeries, downtime, inconvenience, and so much more for no apparent reason. It was only months after that I realized surgery would never fix the issue ... because *it all stemmed from what was going on in my mind and heart.*

I'd be lying if I said my ego hasn't gotten very involved in the process of moving forward after my betrayal. It's been an exhausting back-and-forth between my ego and my highest self. Everything about my ego mocked the idea of forgiveness and building an entirely new relationship with my husband: "What a bunch of garbage. Don't bother." "You're just setting yourself up for more pain. Don't be a sucker." "You're going to let him off the hook that easily?" Then, my highest self would whisper messages of "You know what's best. Trust that."

I'll never forget one experience that really showed how powerful my ego was in making sure I didn't fully forgive—until I caught it red-handed.

Getting back to my feet: Whenever I wore heels, I'd be in so much pain the next day, I always (even after the surgery) had to plan out when and for how long I could have them on.

Now, realizing that foot pain represents an inability, fear, or unwillingness to move forward, it makes perfect sense to have foot issues after my betrayal, right? So, one night, while my husband and I were pretty far along in our "rebuilding a new relationship" stage, the most interesting thing happened. I'd been cautiously rebuilding an entirely new relationship with him, and he'd been consistently and carefully showing me that I'd never have any reason to question anything ever again.

During that day, we'd been busy with the kids, running errands, and doing normal daytime activities. I remember wearing jeans, a T-shirt, and running shoes (it's important to mention, and you'll soon hear why). We'd gone out to dinner—nothing fancy, just a simple Saturday night out. After dinner, there was the briefest moment when I felt totally safe … as if all the hurt, the pain, the anguish, the fear, the doubt, and every other emotion that betrayal creates just vanished. I felt an overwhelming sense of freedom, peace, and trust. It was so unmistakable that I remember exactly where I was when this brief but crystal-clear experience happened. The moment ended. It was a nice night, and I went to sleep.

The next morning, I woke up in the most unbearable pain in both feet—it felt as if I'd danced all night long in six-inch heels. It didn't make any sense at all. I'd worn running shoes during the day and flats the night before. There was absolutely no reason why my feet should have been in all that pain. Then, I realized that there's always more to things than we often realize, so I used one of the practices I'll share with you now to help find some answers.

I started tapping (that's Emotional Freedom Technique [EFT]). Within minutes, I got the clearest message that just made so much sense.

I heard, "Your hard stance keeps you in a hard stance." Meaning, my hard stance (my rigid and unbending viewpoint in refusing to fully forgive and believe I was safe) keeps me in a hard stance (the rigid, unbending, and painful stance that was keeping my feet, along with the rest of my body and mind, in physical, mental, and emotional pain). I felt and experienced firsthand how withholding forgiveness and hanging onto all that pain was keeping me stuck. I was sold, and I worked to quiet my ego and listen to my highest self instead.

Are you rigid or unbending? Is it showing up in body pain that you may be ignoring or medicating? Your body is speaking to you. Are you listening? Is there a nagging pain or a physical reaction stemming from an unresolved emotion?

Here's another example of how the body speaks to us, letting us know that while we may think we're healed, we're using a shield of protection to stay hardened. Be on the lookout to seeing if it reminds you of something similar to what you are experiencing.

A Pain in the Neck

With six out of seven cervical discs pressing on nerves in my neck, it's exhausting, to say the least. Years ago, I remember going to a few doctors who diagnosed me with degenerative disc disease, herniated discs, slipped discs, and even arthritis in my neck. My neck is so inflamed, rigid, and stiff that it's often dangerous to drive, because my range of motion is so limited that I can barely turn my head to look over my shoulder. If I need to see something behind me, my whole body turns, not just my neck.

Some doctors said that surgery is the only option, but with it came a chance of paralysis. Yikes! Other doctors suggested injections (which I tried). I've also tried pain patches, heating pads, numbing creams, Reiki, craniosacral therapy, acupuncture, a neck brace, massage, cupping, and chiropractic sessions (three times a week for eight months), and even bought an inversion table so I can slowly pull the discs away from the nerves and get some relief. (By the way, while some people feel great relief from an inversion table, flipping upside down felt like a bad carnival ride to me.)

So, I've gotten used to walking around like Frankenstein, with my neck locked in position and in pain. But since this amount of constant and chronic pain makes no sense, I always dive deeper.

Let's consider the obvious: stress. Think about it. When we're stressed, we lift and tighten our neck and shoulders. It's as if we're bracing ourselves for impact. While that may be useful in the short term, bracing ourselves for impact 24/7 is telling our bodies that we're under constant attack. So the mind tells the body to prepare for danger, and the body responds by bracing itself. Before long, there's a body-mind loop happening, as the body is conditioned to this response. The mind keeps telling the body, "Ok, since you need all of this protection, I'll keep fighting for you and keep you braced and ready." So the mind tells the body, the body responds, and then the body tells the mind, "Keep it coming," and the mind responds.

Before long, you're in a body-mind stress response where the body and mind are both on high alert.

Barring physical trauma like a car accident or fall, this response is generated by our thoughts and feelings, and the meaning we give to our experiences. Bad posture can contribute to pain as well, so if you're hunched over staring at a screen all day, that's not going to help.

Now let's get to what neck pain energetically represents: rigidity, an unwillingness to go with the flow, overload, too much to deal with, fear, and insecurity. Carrying the weight of the world, something or someone is a "pain in the neck"; inability to let go and/or forgive.

That pretty much described me exactly. So now, I want to share how, so you can take a look to see if that may be what's happening with you, too.

Let's start with rigidity. When life is chaotic, we feel we've lost control. It can be something as simple as too many tasks, demands, obligations, and responsibilities that create a sense of overwhelm. We can feel like we can't keep up with all that's expected of us and the many roles we play. Without any additional meaning, for me, the demands of four kids, six dogs, and maintaining a marriage, home, and thriving business would be enough of a reason to feel like life is spinning out of control.

Now, let's add in a Type A personality and being a double Aries (which I learned astrologically means there's good reason for my intense drive coupled with intense impatience), and it's clear that rigidity would seem like a way to keep me on track and moving toward whatever particular target I had in mind.

Now, let's take going with the flow. I don't know about you, but I think I go with the flow … as long as that flow is what I planned, hoped for, and expected. Then? It's perfectly fine with me ⊠.

Staying with an unwillingness to go with the flow, let's add in fear and insecurity, which are all energetic reasons for neck issues. This has everything to do with the betrayals of my family and husband (for details, it's all in **Trust Again** thepbtinstitute.com/trustagain). Betrayal is such a painful shock to the body, mind, and heart. This was the person (or these were the people) who gave you a sense of safety and security. So when this is the person (or these are the people) who shatter that very sense of safety and security, it's terrifying.

It's terrifying because all the rules, whether spoken or unspoken, have just changed without our awareness or consent. There's no order, only chaos. One minute we feel fine, and the next minute, we don't know our place in the family, in the marriage, in the friendship. Nothing feels safe, predictable, or certain. The person we'd run to for safety IS the one causing the harm. So where do we run? Who can we trust? What do we do?

Our world now feels completely unsafe, unpredictable, and unrelentingly painful. So when we think about how neck pain also can mean an unwillingness to go with the flow, fear, and insecurity, it makes perfect sense if for no other reason than the earth-shattering experience betrayal creates. How do we go with the flow when life as we've known it has just shattered in a million pieces? How can we *not* feel fear and insecurity when our very sense of safety and security has been completely destroyed?

That's exactly how I felt after my betrayal experiences, and if you've gone through it, too, you know that shock, that pain, that uncertainty. Add to that the need to show up to do your work, be there for your kids, and take care of your parents, pets, or whatever other obligations you have. Life is spinning out of control, and we're desperately trying to grab the reins to stop the spinning. While we can get to that place of control, safety, peace, and even transformation, it's easy to see how this type of experience can wreak havoc on our body.

Breaking it down even further, let's take what fear and insecurity can do to the body. When you're in this heightened state of alert, you've ignited the stress response, which then triggers the beginning of stress-related symptoms, illnesses, conditions, and disease. When you're in a constant state of fight/flight/freeze, your body remains on high alert. It's as if you're running for safety 24/7. In the short term, it's a brilliant response, and it's designed to keep you safe and alive. For example, if you were being chased by a wild animal, foaming at the mouth and looking at you like you'd be the perfect dinner, this response is needed. The burst of adrenaline and cortisol enables blood and oxygen to go to the heart, lungs, and limbs, so you can run to safety. The stress response is doing its job, and it gives you the added boost of energy, blood, and oxygen to keep you alive. That's great when you're in a situation like that, but when it's chronic, it's a different story.

When we live in a state of fear and insecurity, the stress response is ignited, and it stays that way. So that burst of energy you needed for the short term is now working full time. Eventually, it's draining your resources and causing a host of issues. Your adrenals crash; your immune system is shot; you don't have the resistance to illness and disease you had when life was under control. You're aging faster and gaining weight (particularly in your mid-section). You're exhausted and anxious.

Because you have to get through your day, you start treating the symptoms. If you're exhausted, you may take something to help you sleep. If you're anxious, you may have a few glasses of wine. If you're lacking in energy, you may use sugar and caffeine for a pick-me-up. This false energy that's being created isn't sustainable, so the cycle continues. The sugar you're adding for additional energy (and comfort) is adding to the weight issue that was triggered by the stress.

New issues seem to pop up. For me, it was arthritis and all kinds of muscle pain, joint pain, and inflammation. So maybe you start taking things for that, too. Nothing is really working. At the root of it is this intense fear and insecurity, because life has just completely rocked you to your core, and you're grasping for control so you can catch your breath and figure it out.

It seems easier to treat the symptoms, because it's a proactive approach, and on some level, that has us feeling like we're taking back control—doing something good with something bad. Yes, treating the symptoms helps a bit, but if we're not getting to the root, it's a temporary solution at best.

The more we treat the symptoms, the further we get away from what caused the symptoms in the first place. The more we dive into the specific issue we see (a gut issue, anxiety, a sleep disorder, joint pain, etc.), the further we get from getting to what's driving the real issue.

Our bodies are telling us that something needs our attention, and instead of listening, we do all we can to squelch that voice. I was as proactive as I could be, going on endless searches to stop the physical pain, but clearly wasn't doing enough to listen to what the emotional pain was trying to say. Looking at it all, it probably would have been a miracle if I hadn't had all that neck pain.

The neck is also tied to one of the chakras—if you're unfamiliar with chakras, they're energetic points on the body. When blocked, out of balance, deficient, or excessive, it impacts us physically, mentally, and emotionally. Well wouldn't you know, communication, self-expression, speaking your truth, inability to speak up, restriction, and keeping things bottled up and contained are all tied to neck issues and to the throat chakra? How perfect is that?! Can you see how it's hard to communicate when life just up-ends itself until you find solid ground after a painful experience? Can you see how navigating through a crisis can leave you in such shock, you can't even find the words to express how you're feeling?

We're never truly healed emotionally when our bodies are crying out to us physically. Instead of being upset or angry at the symptoms popping up, look at them as your bodies way of telling you what needs your attention. Instead of medicating the symptom, get to the root. Instead of ignoring it (my go-to response, because who's got the time or patience to figure all of this out?), find out what every symptom and body pain is trying to tell you.

When your car is low on gas, it lets you know by showing you how much gas is left in the tank. A warning light will come on when something isn't performing the way it's supposed to. You wouldn't ignore the fact that you need to refuel, and you wouldn't put a sticker over the engine light, so you don't see it. Ignoring the real issue (you need gas in the car) will only take you so far—however much gas is left in the tank. "Treating" the engine light by putting a sticker over it only allows for the car to continue to break down. So why is it so obvious when it comes to a car and not when it comes to us?

Our bodies weren't meant to handle the continuous and unrelenting onslaught of emotional upheaval, which leaves a physical toll. Our bodies are the vehicles taking us around to do all we're here to do. If it's "acting up," there's a reason. Listen and truly hear what it's trying to tell you.

So, while I'm doing the work to heal (just like you), apparently, there's lots more to be done. What about you?

What Is Your Body Trying to Tell You?

Take the time to list every symptom, illness, condition, even disease. See how they could be tied to something emotionally challenging or to a belief system that doesn't serve you. Try to see how your body is letting you know you're overwhelmed, sad, hurt, or in need of love, safety, or security. Start to identify the subtle (or not-so-subtle) ways your body is telling you it needs your attention.

For example, how might exhaustion be tied to your running on empty? How might a weight issue be you trying to protect yourself, because it keeps certain expectations or experiences at bay? How might a gut issue be alerting you to something painful for you to "digest, process, and absorb?" How could blurry vision be due to something you don't want to see? How might a skin issue (redness, eczema, and hives, for example) be tied to anxiety, anger, or depression?

How is unresolved trauma, a belief system that no longer serves you, or an outdated expectation showing up in how you look, feel, and live? How is the accumulation of negative beliefs and resignation to "this is as good as it's getting, so I'd better get used to it" showing up in your relationships, your health, and your work?

When you look around, you'll find that your current situation is a living, breathing example of the thoughts you think. Your beliefs got you where you are, so it's going to take a new set of beliefs to get somewhere else. Remember, you may very likely be comfortable and surviving, and if that's your goal, you're doing it. However, if there's a nagging unease—a sense that there's more, and/or a feeling of being bottled, contained, and limited, there's work to do. If you know that the fear or the confrontation waiting for you because of who your changes will impact is holding you back, I'm talking to you. If guilt or lots of "shoulds" are ruling your decisions, I'm talking to you. If being practical is taking over your joy, passion, and purpose, I'm talking to you.

I'm not saying to be reckless or to disregard those depending on your care. I'm saying it's time to put yourself on your own to-do list. We're so conditioned to put everyone else first, as if our needs don't matter. Trust me, I learned this one the hard way more times that I can count. Here's the truth:

The happier you are, the more you have to give, so stop settling for squelched and unmet needs with the hope that they'll go away. Stop settling because it's easier. Stop wishing it were different.

Evolutionary or Revolutionary?

I remember working with someone who said, "My changes need to be evolutionary, not revolutionary." Meaning, she was willing to make small changes that would add up over time versus changes that create a gigantic shakeup to everything and everyone around her. If that's a better approach for you, that's just as effective. Some people need to dive right into the deep end, and others need a more subtle approach—dipping their toe into the water and slowly getting used to the temperature.

Here's an example of how both approaches can work: One of my children is a "dive into the deep end" type of person who's found that incremental approaches aren't nearly as effective as diving in head-first. For example, I remember the year she decided to study abroad in China. She came to us with the idea, all figured out: "It's actually less expensive than being on campus. It's 10 credits, and since my nighttime is your morning, we can Facetime each other then." Well, she researched the entire trip, spoke with everyone she needed to speak with regarding visas, travel, housing, etc. We took her to the airport and trusted that it was a good idea.

After a few days, she was freaking out. "Mom, what the heck was I thinking?! I don't speak a word of Chinese. I have no idea what I'm doing! I'm vegetarian, and I can't even figure out what I'm eating. What did I do?!" I went into full-throttle mom mode: "Give it a few days; I'm sure it's going to be ok."

A week later: "Mom, this is the GREATEST place ever! Everyone is so nice. I know my way around, and there's even a really sweet lady at the fruit stand who cuts up my melon for me. I love it here! I'm so glad I did this." Whew. She's done this so many times, and while I've learned that the freaking out part is temporary, the "revolutionary" approach works best for her and is her go-to style for overcoming fear.

Here's an example of the "evolutionary" approach:

We have members within **The PBT Institute Membership Community** thepbtinstitute.com/join who dip their toe in first. Maybe they do one of the program modules on their own time, or they watch a replay of a class, so they don't have to interact with anyone. After a few weeks, they may attend a live class, but they don't have their cameras on, because that feels too vulnerable and personal. Maybe a week or two later, they attend a live class, their cameras are on, and they're interacting in class and on our forums. They're moving forward, but at a pace that feels gentler and more sustainable for them.

Either will work. The only approach that doesn't work is doing nothing, and since you're reading this, I'm guessing that's not who you are or why you're here.

Moving You Forward

Now, if you're headed toward healing, you may have already worked through lots of these physical, mental, and emotional challenges. You may have created your unique "recipe" for healing based on your specific needs and preferences. You may have looked at a negative set of beliefs or painful experience as something to move through versus something that needs to remain fixed and permanent. You may have already done lots of work around realizing that the behaviors of others have very little to do with you, and it's clear that you're on a path toward growth and transformation. You may have resolved old issues, which has revealed an exciting path you never would have had access to had your experience not happened. Wherever you find yourself, it's perfect.

If you realize you've been stuck, let's get you unstuck, so you can create the level of abundance you deserve. If what you've already done has now given you the confidence to make a bold move, dive into a new direction, or venture into a new arena, that's great too. It's not that we're not supposed to be happy with our progress, it's that we're here to squeeze the juice out of life. If we even take one step toward a better way to think, feel, and live, that's great! No one starts from the same place. We all have our stories, our beliefs, our conditioning, our personalities, and our support (or lack of support) that keeps us stuck or propels us forward. My goal? To inch you closer to the health, relationships, work, and success you deserve. To move you from the Willow to the Cactus, to the Bamboo, and to the Lotus. HealedOrHardenedQuiz.com

There's a difference between running from your past and running toward your future. When we're stuck in a more hardened state, it's often because we're doing all we can to run from our past. We're trying to outrun painful feelings, or we're trying to justify staying exactly where we are. When uncomfortable feelings arise, we try to squelch them or stay ahead of them. Have you noticed that they follow you around like a shadow?

I often share these questions on podcasts and within **The PBT Institute** thepbtinstitute.com/join, because they're very revealing. Take the time to journal these questions to see if there may be something you've been trying to outrun or pretend not to see:

1. Am I numbing, avoiding, and/or distracting myself? If so, how?

2. What am I pretending not to see?

3. What's life going to look like in five to 10 years if I do nothing?

4. What can life look like in five to 10 years if I change now?

Transformation begins when we tell ourselves the truth, and these questions can help you uncover ideas you may now be ready to see. Take your time with these questions, and make the decision that it's time to move forward.

When we're moving toward a more healed state, we're eagerly running toward our future. We get more out of every experience when we're mindful of the present, but we're also fueled with an excitement and curiosity about what's next for us. We're not sure what the future will bring, but we're excited to find out. We're not promised a specific outcome, but we're willing to do the work toward an outcome we'd like. The future seems bright with our conscious and intentional involvement. We're proactive in creating an outcome versus being reactive where we're simply hoping everything goes in a way that works for us. Wherever you are is perfect, because it serves as the baseline of where you're headed. The only goal here is to keep moving forward.

There's no race, because there's no end.

You're deciding on the path and the destination, fueling it with passion and purpose along the way.

Before we leave PART TWO, use any physical symptoms or issues you're experiencing to see if you can trace them back to any emotional roots. Of course, symptoms and conditions can be the result of a physical trauma to the body, an allergic reaction to an ingredient, an overuse injury, and more, so you don't want to disregard other possible reasons for what you're experiencing. It's just that you don't want to *only* view the physical reasons why you may be experiencing a symptom or illness, because very often, it can be traced back to emotional roots.

Are You Taking a Healed or Hardened Stance?

One more thing before leaving PART TWO:

Assess how you feel and the emotions you experience most. Do you lean more toward anger, bitterness, envy, hopelessness, helplessness, sadness, frustration, shame, blame, guilt, and resentment? Or do you lean more toward acceptance, gratitude, inspiration, joy, compassion, empathy, and love? Do you feel justified, righteous, and fearful? Or, do you feel confident, assured, happy, at peace, and curious?

A more hardened person may have a perspective like: "Don't go there. I'm good as long as I don't see that person. I'm fine; just leave it at that. Happy? No, but who is?" "What's the point? It's not worth it."

A more healed person may have a perspective like: "What's next? Yes, it was my experience, but it doesn't define who I am. I experienced that (trauma, painful exchange, abusive behavior, etc.), but I'm not broken, a victim, or damaged goods."

With regard to the cleanup left in the wake of their experience, the more stuck and hardened person can look at it very differently than the person who's determined to move toward healing. The more hardened person can add those physical ailments to the list of "why me," concluding that it's just their bad luck and lot in life to deal with these additional issues, too.

A person with a more flexible viewpoint on the road to healing looks at it much differently. They're seekers and look at symptoms as the body's way of letting us know that something isn't right. They don't blame the body for reacting, but lovingly seek solutions to heal the root cause for the symptom showing up in the first place. They don't neglect the signs; they address them with curiosity and concern. They know that while they may have been hard on themselves in the past, it takes self-compassion and personal power to initiate change.

As we move to PART THREE, I want you to know that I understand the struggle between the many emotions going on inside of you. There may be a desire to let go of the past, yet a comfortable feeling of clinging to negative emotions that are so familiar. There's a drive for something better, yet there's the pull to stay the same. There's the fear of change, yet there's the unhappiness with the present. As all of this swirls around your mind, and it's enough to keep you stuck right where you are. Sometimes, that's perfectly fine. As I mentioned in my first **TEDx: Stop Sabotaging Yourself** www. youtube.com/watch?v=XX30i6nC7ro:

"When the pain of where you are becomes bigger than the fear of the unknown, that's when you jump." So if you're struggling to make sense and meaning out of something, and it's causing symptoms and illness in the process, you're not alone.

Here's an old story of Two Wolves, showing you that the confusion caused by a range of emotions is common:

An old Cherokee is teaching his grandson about life:

"A fight is going on inside me," he said to the boy.

"It is a terrible fight, and it is between two wolves. One is evil— he is anger, envy, sorrow, regret, greed, arrogance, self-pity, guilt, resentment, inferiority, lies, false pride, superiority, and ego."

He continued, "The other is good—he is joy, peace, love, hope, serenity, humility, kindness, benevolence, empathy, generosity, truth, compassion, and faith."

The grandfather said: "The same fight is going on inside you—and inside every other person, too."

The grandson thought about it for a minute and then asked his grandfather: "Which wolf will win?"

The old Cherokee simply replied, "The one you feed."

So, which "wolf" are you feeding? One that's being created by accumulated anger, resentment, and disappointment? One for whom temporary relief comes from blaming others, or by "checking out" by diving into a distraction? Are you feeding the idea that just because someone said or did something hurtful, harmful, or hateful, you must have deserved it? Have you fed yourself that disempowering saying, "Life sucks, and then you die," and has a lack of passion convinced you that it's easier to "kill time" than pursue happiness?

Or are you tending to the signals telling you that acceptance, forgiveness, compassion, and empathy are needed? Are you paying attention to the signs showing you that your energy is best served on your growth versus spending it on staying stuck in the past? Have you realized that competition is killing your joy and celebrating the success of others only enhances your own? Have you realized that emotions like bitterness and shame don't look good on you anymore, and you're ready to drop them like a bad habit? Are you the Willow or Cactus in Stage Two or Stage Three? Or are you moving toward the Bamboo and Lotus in Stage Four or Five? HealedOrHardenedQuiz.com

There's no right or wrong here. Anything you've done, thought of, and believed in up until now was the result of all you had access to. Everyone acts from their current level of consciousness, and the best part about all of it is that it's not something that's fixed and unable to be changed. We're not headed toward healing, because we can't find contentment around where we are. We choose to heal because we're listening to the subtle nudging from our soul telling us to play bigger. Although it's so temping to listen to the loud voice of our ego claiming it knows what's best for us, it's the calm, insightful words from our soul that feel like they hold so much more promise. I'm choosing to turn down the noise of my ego, so I can hear that gentle voice of my soul, urging me toward something it knows I'm meant for. Which voice will you choose to listen to?

PART THREE
Heal It

The Chef's Daughter:

The Story:

There once was a girl who was complaining to her dad that her life was so hard, and she didn't know how she would get through all of her struggles. She was tired, and she felt like as soon as one problem was solved, another would arise.

Being a chef, the girl's father took her into his kitchen. He boiled three pots of water of equal size. He placed potatoes in one pot, eggs in another, and ground coffee beans in the final pot.

He let the pots sit and boil for a while, not saying anything to his daughter.

He turned the burners off after twenty minutes and removed the potatoes from the pot and put them in a bowl. He did the same with the boiled eggs. He then used a ladle to scoop out the boiled coffee and poured it in a mug. He asked his daughter, "What do you see?"

She responded, "Potatoes, eggs, and coffee."

Her father told her to take a closer look and touch the potatoes. After doing so, she noticed they were soft. Her father then told her to break open an egg. She acknowledged the hard-boiled egg. Finally, he told her to take a sip of the coffee. It was rich and delicious.

After asking her father what all of this meant, he explained that each of the three food items had just undergone the exact same hardship—twenty minutes inside of boiling water.

However, each item had a different reaction.

The potato went into the water as a strong, hard item, but after being boiled, it turned soft and weak.

The egg was fragile when it entered the water, with a thin outer shell protecting a liquid interior. However, after it was left to boil, the inside of the egg became firm and strong.

Finally, the ground coffee beans were different. Upon being exposed to boiling water, they changed the water to create something new altogether.

He then asked his daughter, "Which are you? When you face adversity, do you respond by becoming soft and weak? Do you build strength? Or do you change the situation?"

The moral of the story: Life is filled with experiences that give us an opportunity to learn, grow, and evolve. It's filled with twists and turns, ups and downs, wins and losses, starts and stops. Adversity and challenges are simply a part of life. While we'd rather not face challenges, they're not necessarily a bad thing. Handling adversity and overcoming obstacles is what leads to courage, strength, growth, and transformation.

You choose how you respond to every challenge you face. You can let it keep you stuck, or you can learn from it, and it can make you stronger, wiser, and better. Facing challenges also gives us the opportunity to learn important lessons we never would have learned if that challenge didn't come our way.

Easy Now, Hard Later

There's a saying I use that my clients from over 30 years ago still remember. It applies to every area of life, and it's a great way to catch yourself to see how you're choosing to react to something that needs your attention. Whether you use this mantra as it relates to losing weight, a relationship issue, or a work challenge, it'll work regardless of the topic. Ready?

> *Hard now, easy later. Easy now, hard later.*
> *Take your pick, because it's going to be one of those two.*

Here's an example of how each would look—let's take "easy now, hard later" first as it relates to weight loss:

Easy now (I want the cookies). Hard later (I can't button my pants).

Hard now (I want the cookies, but I'm going to have an apple instead). Easy later (look at me! I look great!).

Here's another example regarding relationships:

Easy now (we need to have that conversation, but it's awkward, so forget it). Hard later (we're not communicating and drifting apart).

Hard now (I really don't want to have that awkward conversation, but it's necessary). Easy later (wow, I'm so glad we cleared up that misunderstanding and have a better plan going forward).

See? It works for just about every topic I can think of. What do I see most people choosing? Easy now, hard later. But when it comes to healing, losing weight, or getting to the other side of a challenging issue, which do we *need* to choose? Hard now, easy later.

That's not saying that this is something we're always conscious of. Sometimes, we think we're doing the "hard now" part while what we're really doing is keeping ourselves busy so we don't have to do the really uncomfortable stuff. While all of the "doing" is great, it can be a distraction, actually preventing us from our transformation. You see, transformation begins when you tell yourself the truth. Here's what I mean:

I was working with one of our members within **The PBT Institute** thepbtinstitute.com/join, and she was telling me all about the self-care strategies she was doing. She was going on and on about how she was eating well, exercising, getting enough sleep, taking supplements, etc. Sounds great, right? It's all about the intention behind it.

In her case, all of those self-care strategies, while great to include in a healthy lifestyle, were healthy distractions. She had been using them to prevent herself from connecting with her heart, because that's where the real challenge was hidden.

So after complimenting her on her hard work to implement new, healthy habits, I asked her to stop. She was a bit taken aback, but I wanted to get to the root of the issue, and after coaching for 30 years, there are a few things I've learned to notice. Her changes were keeping her from paying attention to her soul, to her heart, to what she wants, and from where she's meant to go. So I said, "All of that sounds great—it really does. It's also coming entirely from your head. It's like you're saying and doing everything you're supposed to say, and if you do all of these things, you're supposed to be happy and have a great life."

She tilted her head, leaned in, and said, "Um, I don't get it. Yeah, I mean, I feel better. That's good, right?" "Of course it's good, and if the underlying issue was that you were trying to improve your health, that would be great. But that's not what's nagging at your heart."

She was listening. "So, forget all the 'shoulds.' I'm not here to judge anything you're doing and not doing. While it all sounds nice, it's all coming from your head. What does your heart have to say?"

"I don't know."

"Pretend you do, because whenever anyone says they 'don't know,' what that often means is, 'You've gone as far as I'll let you. What's next is off limits.'"

"Ok, so what I want is …"

And out came a beautiful story of triumph, love, resilience, forgiveness, passion, and purpose. She stopped, and I encouraged her to share more. More details, more insights, more awareness, more connecting with who she's here to become. More time to see that beautiful version of her that's been so patiently waiting to show up. More time to create a felt sense of what it would feel like to live, breathe, act, think, and react as the version of her she could see so clearly.

I wanted her to have such a bright, vibrant, and clear picture, so it would imprint itself on her body, mind, and heart. And the more time she had to create the full picture and scene, the more beautiful it was. I got chills; she did, too. I held back tears. She did, too. Then she said, "Wow. That's me. That's really me." So I asked, "What do you need to do to become that version of you?" She said, "I don't know. Wait, um, I can take a first step. Something to get started." "Exactly! She's been waiting a long time for you, and she'll give you every answer you need. Move toward her. It doesn't matter if it's in the smallest, most incremental amounts each day, but there she is. She's waiting."

Do you see? The health changes were great, but focusing on the "doing" was a distraction from figuring out who she was "being." Now that she had her target, the "doing" could be so much more strategic, as she was able to take actions that would bring her closer to the version of herself she was ready to become.

I find that it's often so much easier to do the "doing." When we do, there's a sense of accomplishment—we can check things off our list; we can feel productive, and look at a list of tasks we've done and consider it a job well done. I know that so well, because that was my shield for decades.

With four kids, six dogs, and a thriving business, I had a list a mile long of daily tasks. Nothing at the time made me feel better than "getting it all done and then some." I'd take such pride in hearing how well I was managing it all, how easy I made it look, and how much I was able to accomplish. Those compliments fed me, and I wore the mask of "busy mom doing it all," because back then, I questioned my value and worth if I just took it easy. Somehow, the more I did equaled the more value I had, which by the way, is the perfect recipe for burnout (been there, done that a few times).

When I realized I had that mask on, I struggled with it for a long time. "Lazy" and "slacker" were some of the words and labels that felt like nails on a blackboard, so I went so far the other way, I'd never hear them being said about me. Somehow, I believed that the more I did, the more valuable I was.

Think about it. If your value is derived by all you do, what happens when you stop doing those things?

Who are you without all the external measures that show you and others your worth? Who are you without the car, clothes, jewelry, awards, degrees, and extravagant lifestyle? Who are you if a life of meaning and purpose is dependent on how much you do versus who you are?

In this section, I'm going to share stories from some of our incredible Certified PBT Coaches who teach daily classes within our community thepbtinstitute.com/join. They've bravely contributed their stories so you can see what it looked like as they moved from one stage to the next. They're going to walk you through their individual experiences through **The Five Stages**, so you can see what trauma and transformation can look like. You'll see how they've gone from Willow to Cactus to Bamboo to Lotus, moving from Stage Two to Stage Three to Stage Four to Stage Five. Through their example, you'll also see if your experience has kept you stuck in a particular stage, or if you're slowly and steadily moving forward.

We'll also dive into some tools, strategies, and solutions that may be just what you need to kickstart your healing as you move from hardened to healed. Want to ensure you keep moving forward and don't get stuck? Want to know what'll move you the quickest and most effectively?

Willingness.

The more willing you are, the less resistant you'll be. As long as you remain willing to move forward, the next steps will eventually reveal themselves. Cling to the old, and that's exactly what you'll continue to have. Decide to be a willing participant in creating a healthier or more desirable future, and you'll be open to the ideas, downloads, and opportunities likely to come your way.

So let's first dive into a few stories of trauma to transformation from Certified PBT Coaches Elizabeth, Josh, and Michelle, detailing their move through **The Five Stages from Betrayal to Breakthrough**. I'll give you an abbreviated version of my story through the stages, too (a more in-depth and detailed version is found in **Trust Again**: thepbtinstitute.com/trustagain). Then, it's your turn. With examples as reference points, you'll see where you are and decide where you want to go. I'll offer you ideas that members within our community have found helpful and that I've personally seen change how we look, feel, and live. Lots to cover, so let's dive in.

Stories of Transformation

The Challenges and Gifts of the Betrayal Experience: Looking for Love in All the Wrong Places

By **Elizabeth R Kipp**

Lead Up to Betrayal: "I Never Saw It Coming."

All I ever remember wanting more than anything else as a child was love from my mother. It was more than "wanting," because "wanting" implies a craving for something. For me, this wish was deeply primal. It was a desire for deep connection, and in my mother's case, it was profound. It became a mission for me—a quest for love in a world where I felt love was most often void or twisted into a kind of material expression. So often, I did not feel my need for connection satisfied.

My mother suffered from untreated bipolar disorder, chronic pain, and alcohol addiction. Her behavior was erratic and unpredictable, except for one thing: I could predict that she would rage at me at least once each day. I just never knew when it would happen. So, I learned to be hypervigilant. I learned to be quiet and not express myself either vocally or emotionally. These tendencies helped to keep me safe, and they impressed deeply into my nervous system.

In the back of my childhood mind, I always held out hope that if I could just figure out "the right way to be," my mother might not point her fury at me, but instead open her heart to me with love. I just can't remember that ever happening.

From the beginning of my life, you could say I experienced betrayal from my mother, because she broke an unspoken rule in our relationship: to love and protect me as her child. In my laser-focused desire for my mother's love, I never saw her betrayal coming. It did not even seem within the realm of possibility in my innocent child's mind.

Stage One: The Setup—Disproportionately Prioritizing Physical and Mental Versus Emotional and Spiritual Needs

When I was thirteen years old, my parents divorced. I lived with my father for two years and then moved in with my mother. We were preparing dinner in the kitchen one evening, and all of a sudden, my mother rushed at me in a rage with a large chopping knife and pushed it up against the bare skin of my neck. I had no idea what I had done to provoke this act. I was terrified. I stood rooted in shock as if suspended in time. As I waited to die, I remember thinking that I must be a horrible person, since my mother was taking me out. As I stood still, my mother facing me with the knife-edge pressed against the skin of my neck, I felt an unknown surge of energy enter the top of my head that then coursed into my neck, through my arms, and out my hands. The force of this energy seemed to push my mother back away from me. She took three steps directly back and dropped the knife onto the floor. Then she turned and walked slowly, almost catatonically, to the far end corner of the living room. She collapsed onto the floor and fell asleep.

I stood stunned and felt entirely out of balance. I knew I had to act to find a sense of safety, but I was unsure what to do. I called my father, who lived fifty miles away, and told him what had just happened. I hoped he would come and get me. He had another plan.

"Stay there for the night. In the morning, pack a bag, and tell your mother that you are spending the weekend with me. Leave as if nothing has happened."

Once again, I was shocked. I couldn't believe that my father was not getting in his car and immediately driving up to rescue me from my mother, who was so obviously unstable and threatening my life. So, now I felt a second betrayal, this time from my father. Who was going to keep me safe? It turned out that it was my job to keep myself safe, because those closest to me were not going to do it. Not feeling safe was the culmination of a pattern I had experienced my whole life but had not understood until that moment. I often felt that I was not safe at home, but I had no one with whom to share this worry.

I had left my old school and my childhood friends to live in a new city with my mother. I had been enrolled in a new school and was only two weeks into the school year when my mother attacked me. I felt estranged from my old friends and had not made any new friends yet, so I had no friends to turn to for help. I felt trapped in my body and mind and did not know how to escape the intense feelings and thoughts I had experienced. I did not have a haven to turn to—not my parents or friends. Even my mind and body did not seem a protected refuge for me.

I did what I could to think my way through the situation and tried to ignore the trembling in my body. It seemed like my logical mind was the only way I had to navigate my path going forward. I felt the presence of Spirit, but only barely. I didn't realize until much later that Spirit was the mysterious force that entered through the top of my head and propelled my mother and her knife against my throat away from me.

Stage Two: Breakdown of the Body, Mind, and Worldview

When the following day arrived, I packed a small suitcase and said goodbye to my mother.

"I'm going to Daddy's for the weekend. See you later, Mom," was the most I could muster.

I walked to the car and got behind the wheel. My brain was so foggy that I wondered if I would be able to find my way home fifty miles away. I said a prayer and hoped it would be answered. As I drove out of the driveway, tears streamed down my face. What would become of me? What would become of my mother? Did what just happened really happen? Already, I denied the traumatic event I had just experienced.

Blessedly, I arrived at my father's house safely. I started crying again as I brought the car to a halt. No one was there to greet me at the front door. My stepsisters were not at home. My brother was away at college. My father was up in his bedroom.

I walked up the stairs to my father's room and asked if I could enter.

"Hi, Daddy. I'm here. Can I come up?"

"Are you ok?" he asked.

Assuming he was referring to my physical well-being, even though I was shuddering inside, I replied, "Yes."

He turned to the telephone and called my mother.

"Liz is not coming back," he said.

My father held the phone away from his ear and into the air. I could hear my mother scream her raging anger at my father. I don't remember any of her words, but I sure remember the energy she projected into the telephone. My father's phone call was the only consequence my mother experienced for her attack on me.

I turned, utterly dejected, and went to my bedroom, collapsing on my bed.

I had no idea where I would find support to help me get through my shock. What followed was silence on my father's part. My mother's attempt on my life was never discussed or acknowledged again in my family. It was like it never happened.

I learned that asking for help was not an option for me. Since my parents were unable to deal with their own emotions, they were not available to help me process mine. I learned that I could not trust the people closest to me.

After a while, I began to doubt myself and wondered if I had imagined the whole thing. My body undeniably held the fallout from the trauma. I was frightened and did not know anyone I could turn to for help. The world became a hostile and forsaken place for me.

I had suffered from irritable bowel syndrome throughout my life. It became much more pronounced at this time.

Stage Three: Survival Instincts Emerge

I lived by my wits and in Stage Three for a long time. There had been no consequences for any of the betrayal experiences that happened. I was afraid to say anything to anyone about it, because I would be even more of an outcast in the family than I already was. My mother refused to admit that she had attacked me. My father would not speak about it. Their denial of that night's truth in the kitchen also contributed to my prolonged experience in Stage Three. Finally, I did everything I could to distract myself from facing the horror of my experience and the feelings I harbored about it. I dove into my schoolwork and volunteered after school. I made myself so busy doing things that I went to bed each night exhausted, so I didn't have to feel.

I wondered if I would ever be able to trust anyone again. And in my denial of my experience, I wondered, since I couldn't trust myself to admit my own experiences, if I would be able to truly trust myself.

I lived with chronic pain and concurrent addiction to prescription medication for decades, resulting from these unresolved traumas from my childhood. I suffered from codependence and boundary issues in relationships.

Stage Four: Finding and Adjusting to a New Normal

I was determined that something good would result from my betrayal experience. I just didn't know what that was going to be. I went on with my life. I made new friends. I even got married and became a mother. Once I started my own family, I felt more liberated from my birth family's influence. I began to feel safer in the world, because my husband was a caring, gentle, yet strong and reliable man. I began to relax more. I felt more balanced in the world. I turned toward loving and serving my husband and son. I tried to keep in touch with my mother, but our relationship remained tenuous. I did my best to connect with her, especially because of my son, but it wasn't easy. We both had so much unresolved wounding that it made an authentic connection almost impossible. We stayed estranged from each other.

Stage Five: Healing, Rebirth, and a New Worldview

I entered a pain-management program where I detoxed off the prescription medication. I had the opportunity to do some adversity therapy around my betrayal experience. I saw so clearly how my parents did the best they could, living by their wits, and did not have the healing trauma tools that I was given.

After my mother's death, I learned that as a baby, she had witnessed her father try and murder her mother. She never had an opportunity to process or heal from this trauma, so she carried it with her until the end.

I realized that my mother was ultimately my teacher of compassion. She taught me to look inside myself for love rather than to others. I realized that in my quest for love, I had actualized a dream my mother was never able to access. In my search for love from my mother, I found the eternal love that lives inside me—a profound spiritual teaching.

My chronic pain life dissolved into an experience of ease and inner peace. My nervous system's hypervigilant pattern gradually shifted into a normalized stress response. My yoga and Chi Gong practices were instrumental in helping to return my stress response to health.

Later, I went into Dr. Debi Silber's **Post Betrayal Transformation** program thepbtinstitute.com/join and found even more healing and grounding in my life. I was so impressed with her process that I became a Certified PBT Coach in the hopes of helping others discover the same kind of profound healing that I had experienced. It is my great honor to provide this service to others.

One Addict's Betrayal Trauma Story

By **Joshua Shea**

Stage One: The Setup—Disproportionately Prioritizing Physical and Mental Versus Emotional and Spiritual Needs

When you wake up in the dark on some cold floor, pretty sure that you're naked, fumbling for the doorknob, you're just not thinking about betrayal trauma. You're just wondering why this black cloud keeps following you around.

And this was my life for too many years.

Stage Two: Breakdown of the Body, the Mind, and the Worldview

At the age of 12, in 1988, I discovered hardcore pornography. Two years later, at a wedding, I got drunk for the first time. For the next 25 years, respectively, I didn't bother with too much self-analysis or deep probing of inner turmoil. I was just an addict. I could simply fire-up the Internet, pour myself a giant tumbler of Red Bull and tequila, and pretend that whatever storm had been raging inside of me since childhood wasn't actually there. Sure, I had to lie about the severity of the alcoholism, and I was like a master magician creating the illusion that I had no problems with pornography.

Stage Three: Survival Instincts Emerge

On April 1, 2014, I had my last drink and checked myself into rehab for alcoholism. After a brush with the law, the desertion of my business partners, and a family that was fed up with years of lies, I agreed to get help. I thought that I could spend 28 days in the Southern California sun, play along with the program enough to get a certificate that would impress the judge who was going to decide my legal fate, and then simply rebuild my professional life when I returned home.

I'd had my license for 20 years when I entered rehab. I knew there were weeks toward the end that I'd driven drunk three or four times. I also knew there were times where it only happened once or twice a month. I settled on 1.5 times per week for those 20 years. It didn't sound like much until I did the math. The total was 1,560 times. Even if I overestimated by 25%, it still meant I'd driven drunk over 1,000 times. I felt a wave of shame, embarrassment, and fear—because I knew how many times I'd had passengers with me—including my children—and a light went on. People who were not problem drinkers could not say they drove drunk over 1,000 times in their life. Many people I knew could count on one hand. The message was received, and I began paying attention.

Stage Four: Finding and Adjusting to a New Normal

My stint wasn't 28 days. All told, I spent 70 days in Palm Springs, with the last couple weeks being especially eye-opening, because my caseworker had me start meeting with a Certified Sex Addiction Therapist off campus. He'd recognized issues under the surface relating to potential abuse early in my life and also heard me mention pornography enough to know that he was out of his league. Hence, the referral.

I only spent around 10 hours with this marvelous CSAT, but he helped me realize that pornography addiction was a real condition, and he showed me enough statistical data about it to convince me those faded memories of abuse as a child suddenly didn't seem like a figment of my imagination.

I left California understanding that there was much work to do in maintaining my sobriety when I returned home following rehab, but there was just as much work to do to uncover the story of what happened to me at the hands of a babysitter in the late 1970s and early 1980s.

Over the next three years, I read as much as I could find about pornography addiction, attended hundreds of hours of one-on-one therapy, and returned to inpatient rehabilitation in Texas. Despite not having looked at pornography in over a year when I attended, I knew they could help me get to the core of my issues. Now that I had begun mining my deepest soul, I was on a quest to figure out the complex answer to a seemingly simply question: How did I end up this way?

I first heard the words "betrayal trauma" in the closing days of that seven-week rehab stay. I knew of two types of trauma at that point: the kind you got when you hit your head too hard, and the kind you have after going to into shock. Little did I knew what it really meant, or the fact that I could trace my addictions right back to those two words. Betrayal trauma: there was the answer to my question.

Stage Five: Healing, Rebirth, and a New Worldview

When we talk about needing to get unstuck from our false beliefs, being introduced to the concept of betrayal trauma was one of the biggest steps in getting unstuck that I needed. With years of ongoing therapy and study since learning of betrayal trauma, I have come to recognize that most addicts are probably victims of betrayal trauma, but did not get exposed to proper mental health treatment in time, so they discovered negative ways to cope.

Obviously, I had strong feelings toward the woman who abused me. No child should go through the mental, emotional, or sexual ordeal that I did for several years at this "caregiver's" house. I didn't recognize it until therapy, but there were behaviors, like never driving by her home, that I perpetuated for years during my addictions. The one time I saw her at a store when I was about 15, my mom recalls me running in the other direction. In the late '90s, when she told me this former babysitter died, her follow-up was, "Why are you smiling?" I didn't realize I was.

This "caregiver" scared me into keeping my mouth shut, but for years, a deep part of me wondered how my parents could not tell what was happening to me and my younger brother when we were at this woman's house five days a week. We cried when they left in the morning and leapt into their arms in the late afternoon upon pick-up. Wasn't it obvious? It wasn't until I finally got the courage to tell my parents what happened as part of my recovery that my mother said, "I'm so sorry. You never think something like this is happening to your child. You're supposed to keep your child safe." She broke down crying, and it relieved a lot of the betrayal, because I could tell she was genuinely sorry for the inadvertent neglect.

Recovery from my addictions has been a wonderful road. No longer do I wake up in strange places missing half of my clothes. Nor do I waste hours sitting in front of the computer, hoping the next picture makes me feel better, or that the next swig of alcohol will drown whatever pain is inside.

Recovery from betrayal trauma has been even better. I don't walk around angry, sad, confused, frustrated, and ready for a negative encounter around every corner. I've learned to drop resentments, but also face the fact that within my betrayal trauma and addictions, I deeply hurt a lot of people, like the ones who were in the car when I was driving drunk. I don't think if I hadn't worked on the betrayal trauma that I would have been successful in recovery. I needed to figure out why I became the person I did—a person who could become a double-addict. The answer was found in recovering from betrayal trauma.

From Trauma to Transformation

By **Michelle Silva**

They say hindsight is 20/20. Perfect vision in looking backward over your life. You can see all the mistakes, sorrows, and pains from an entirely different perspective. So many things that didn't make any sense at the time now have perfect clarity once more information comes to light, whether that be someone's disclosure, or your own ability to see things as they really were and are because of your own growth and development.

I am now able to look back over my life and realize that betrayal started very early for me … almost at my birth.

Apparently, I started out as a very happy child. My mother told stories of taking me to the grocery store and having the cashiers fight over who got to check us out, because they all loved me, calling me "Little Miss Sunshine."

Already, I held dark secrets, however—secrets that the neighborhood boys and my daddy told me never to tell a soul, especially mommy. They warned she'd never like me anymore if I told. So I endured, and kept those dark secrets for many years.

One day, my mother just disappeared. I couldn't understand why she would abandon me like that—I hadn't told the secrets. Maybe I just wasn't loveable, and I didn't matter.

My father remarried immediately. I was regularly beaten by both my father and stepmother, once just because, "You look so much like your mother, I wish I could kill you." Dissociation became my best friend. If I wasn't "in there," I didn't have to feel. My mind would go somewhere peaceful and safe while my body was being abused.

At 18, I went to college, got a job, and tried to live my life to the best of my ability. I had no idea how to make good choices, as I had never been allowed to make choices for myself, and I'm afraid I did it quite badly. At 19, I was married, and at 20, I was a mother. Of course, I chose an abusive spouse, as that was what I was used to. The marriage lasted 18 months before I left for my daughter's sake. I did not want her to grow up as I had.

In an effort to understand why my life was so painful and why other people seemed to be happy without the kinds of problems I had, I began to study psychology. I was fascinated by it, hoping that I would be able to make better choices with my newfound knowledge.

My best friend's brother—who I thought was pretty nifty—told her that nobody would want "used merchandise with a child." So when a guy I had known casually for a few years asked me to marry him, I jumped at the chance, certain that no one else would take care of me and my child. I didn't know I could take care of myself. That marriage lasted 12 years, adding two more children. I finally left for the sake of my children. I didn't want them to believe abuse was a normal way of life.

Through the years, I had worked with counselors, constantly learning and improving myself. I continued my self-study, and felt I was in a much better place. It no longer hurt so much to be me. I had begun modeling, and my confidence was quite high. I was self-employed and made decent money. I knew I could take care of my children by myself, and I could be happy. I didn't NEED a man, and I was determined not to marry, ever again.

Three years later, I met the man of my dreams. The attraction we felt toward each other was overwhelming and breathtaking. I was actually irritated, because I was happy with my life, and a man was inconvenient, but I felt he was a blessing. Our courtship was so fast. After one date, we were inseparable. I was skeptical at first, looking for telltale signs that he was just like everybody else I'd ever known.

I actually heard a voice say, "It's ok; he will never deliberately hurt you." With what I felt was Divine assurance, I decided to trust him and opened my heart to him completely. I held nothing back, giving him full access to my inner soul. Within two months, we were engaged, and five months later, we were married. We settled into a happy routine of wedded bliss. He adopted my children, and we added another one to the crew.

Through the years, we had our ups and downs, but I figured that was normal. After all, there's opposition in all things, so we had to have some rough spots in addition to the sweetness of our relationship. I believed that's how two people grow in a marriage. They work through the challenges together and become closer and stronger together.

We dealt with raising children with four very different personalities and all the challenges that brings up. My mother developed Alzheimer's, and we moved her in with us for three years before placing her in a nursing home. We went through loss of employment more than once, and we moved a lot, but through it all, we were affectionate and loving, and stuck by each other.

I felt like I had arrived. I had a good life. I had an amazing family, and I was a very successful Trauma Coach. Little did I know what was in store.

Stage One: The Set Up—Disproportionately Prioritizing Physical and Mental Versus Emotional and Spiritual Needs

About two years before our youngest son graduated from high school, something changed between my husband and me. I could never put my finger on it. It was just a vague discomfort, a flinching, when he would say things that were out of character for him. Normally, he was kind, but he began making comments that really hurt about my competence, about my weight, about the way I ran the household, about how unqualified he thought I was to be running a business. I knew we were all under a great deal of stress trying to make ends meet, caring for my mother, supporting our son who was having some struggles, and maintaining relationships with our family members who had gone out into the world to start their own lives, as well as that of his family of origin, so I made allowances for his behavior. He's tired, or stressed—it's been a long day, etc. Though not quite as physically affectionate as we had been, I chalked that up to being married for over 20 years, and therefore, normal.

I was trying to care for my business, my mother, the family, the household, and also write a book. He was trying to establish his new career in a new area. I suggested we take one weekend a month and go somewhere, so we could refuel our marriage, but somehow, he could never take the time off. I knew he was working hard, so I let it go, though it made me terribly sad. Things would get better once he was established, I was sure. He became short-tempered and would start random disagreements that went around and around in circles, with nothing being settled. I felt like I was walking on eggshells, and our son would frequently ask, "What's wrong with dad?"

If I asked him what was wrong, he always said, "Nothing," though the tone he said it in and his body language told another story. I would follow him into another room, begging for him to talk to me. I told him I felt that he didn't even like me, anymore. This was interspersed with some of the most tender and loving moments of my life. I was always so grateful for those moments, and felt that everything would be ok; we were just going through a rough patch. I thought I must be imagining things, because I believed he would never deliberately hurt me.

Four significant events happened in very quick succession. My father died, and though I hadn't seen him for over 30 years, I had a terrible episode of PTSD that lasted about a week. As long as he was alive, he was a pin on a map, and I knew where he was. Once he died, however, I didn't know where he was. I stepped into my shower one morning and flipped out. Was he in there with me?

Shortly thereafter, I was diagnosed with uterine cancer, and had to go through surgery and treatment for that. I had terrifying hallucinations from the pain medications, so I had to recover using only Advil and Tylenol.

After six years of caring for my mother, she passed away.

Five months later, my husband began a business partnership with a woman against my wishes. I begged him not to, and he said I was jealous, suspicious, and didn't trust him. Trembling all over, I said, "Ok, I'll trust you."

After all, I reminded myself, he would never deliberately hurt me.

Stage Two: Breakdown of the Body, the Mind, and the Worldview

After the formation of the partnership, my husband began staying out very late. He got emoji-filled texts from his partner late at night. People in my small town began telling me how sorry they were that this was happening to me—that they could all see what was going on. Three weeks later, my husband told me that he no longer loved me and wanted a divorce. I still wanted to trust him, and I defended him for months. Everyone must be wrong—he would never have an affair—I still believed he would never deliberately hurt me. Days after our divorce was final, she left her husband, and they moved in together.

I thought I was going to die. I felt like a steamroller had parked on my chest. With each pump of my heart, I could feel cortisol (called the death hormone) pumping through my body. I lost 35 pounds in three weeks. I couldn't hold food down and was in a perpetual state of nausea. My heart hurt so badly, I couldn't breathe. I had broken-heart syndrome. Recent research shows the symptoms can go on for much longer than originally thought. I was in shock, and came down with pneumonia three separate times. I couldn't stop crying and would wake screaming from a troubled sleep. I was suicidal, with a plan in place.

Thank goodness I found the Post Betrayal Transformation Institute—my lifeline. I dug in and did the work.

Stage Three: Survival Instincts Emerge

I do not remember two whole years. Somehow, I managed to give a TEDx talk just a few months after my betrayal, but there are huge holes in my memory. I see pictures with me in them, with no recollection of having been somewhere or what I was doing there. My children and therapist were actually frightened for me.

I fought valiantly to survive. I tried everything to grow my business, as there were financial betrayals in the divorce, as well, and I had to provide for myself. I remember one day just sitting in a puddle on the couch. I asked myself, "Michelle, do you want this betrayal to be the end of your story? Do you want your grandkids to say, 'Grandma was never the same after the betrayal'? Do you want your kids to shake their heads sadly at who you might have been?" My answer was a resounding "NO!"

The first thing I needed to address was my health. After having lost all that weight, my body went the other direction and swelled up like a balloon. My skin felt like it was going to burst. I checked myself into a health clinic in Switzerland, where my doctor put her hands on her hips, and in broken English, said, "Michelle, you love him, yes. He is not worth your life!" For two weeks, she did everything in her power to put me on the path to restored health. I was determined to live—not just survive, but live.

Stage Four: Finding and Adjusting to a New Normal

The months that followed saw a rise in the number of clients I regularly met with, both in person and through the PBT Institute. I discovered that my experiences during this betrayal actually sharpened my skills as a Trauma Coach. Betrayal trauma is nothing like any other kind of trauma, and though I have had so many betrayals in my lifetime, this one was so much different. Because I had opened my heart so completely and trusted without question, I was more vulnerable than I ever had been before. In addition, I have now had a great deal of experience with narcissists, and that expertise has been a boon to many people.

I discovered that I could successfully support myself. I had true friends, and all my needs were comfortably being met. The obsessive thinking became less troublesome, and while I wouldn't use the word "happy" to describe myself, I felt like my new normal was going to be ok.

Stage Five: Healing, Rebirth, and a New Worldview

I seriously wondered if I would ever reach this stage, and for several years, I couldn't even imagine what it would look like. I did writing exercises around what my life might look like, but my reality was so different.

Many years ago, I was in a workshop when Jack Canfield said, "Always end your prayers or affirmations with the phrase, 'If not this, then something better,' because that lets God or the Universe know that you're open to receiving whatever blessings they want to bring into your life."

For decades, I have wanted to open an office where I would meet with clients. I have recently completed certification in Vibroacoustic Therapy, which is an amazing tool, coupled with the energy therapies such as Reiki that I have used for thirty years to help my clients overcome their limiting beliefs, pains, and traumas. My own limiting beliefs, as well as life circumstances in the past, prevented that from happening.

Until now.

I just opened that office! Even though I have been hiding out for the past four years as I worked on my own healing, avoiding going downtown or being seen at all for fear of running into my ex or the mistress, my new office is in the center of town where I am highly visible. I'm writing articles for the Local's Guide, which goes to all households in the city. My picture and a description of my services are in plain sight.

The testimonials I get from my clients bring me to tears. As painful as my life has been, if I had not had these experiences, I would not be able to serve others the same way I am able to now.

I "knew" I would never marry again, and I was perfectly happy with that. I was happy with me. Dr. Debi talks about when you truly heal, you vibrate at a different level, and you attract a different kind of person than you ever have before. I know it sounds cliché, but I was guided, kicking and screaming in protest, to a very special man. God and the Universe made it very clear that we are meant to take the next part of our life journey together.

Never say "never."

I'm not foolish enough to think I have "arrived." Nobody every arrives, and I know there will be more challenges as long as I live, but thanks to loving and supportive people and the brilliance of Dr. Debi Silber and her program thepbtinstitute.com/join, I can certainly thrive.

My Story Through the Stages

Since you already know lots about my story (and the full story is in **Trust Again**), I'm going to keep it brief, showing you how it looks through The Five Stages. This way, you can easily see yourself in a particular stage.

Stage One: The Set Up—Disproportionately Prioritizing Physical and Mental Versus Emotional and Spiritual Needs

I was so busy managing a big family, business, and household, the goal was simply to get it all done. I loved my role as a busy mom, but it took all I had to manage the many details of my hectic schedule. Feed the kids, take them to their clubs and events, manage the six dogs, manage the house, see my clients, grow my business, make time for my husband, and find time for at least a short workout and quick, healthy meals. The day would end, and I'd do it all over again.

Stage Two: Shock, Trauma: The Breakdown of the Body, the Mind and the Worldview

I found out about my husband's betrayal. My world was rocked, my heart was shattered, and I was frozen. I didn't want to believe it, but there it was, and the truth hurt … a lot. I had him leave the house, and I used up every ounce of energy just to deal with the kids, dogs, and my clients. It was a blur. I could barely get out of bed, but knowing I had to take care of the kids and dogs, and knowing I had to be there for my clients, pushed me past what I ever thought I could handle. I don't remember much about those days. I remember doing all I could to be there for the kids, while letting them know I wasn't at my best and needed some grace if I wasn't there for them in the way they needed. I was too embarrassed and ashamed to tell my friends, so I struggled and suffered in silence. My health was crashing, and I couldn't sleep. My mind was racing, going to dark places that I couldn't find my way out of. The situation left me feeling helpless and hopeless, and the future felt bleak.

Stage Three: Survival Instincts Emerge

If I don't get my head together, this will kill me. That was the realization I had from the emergency room after a panic attack. I was hooked up to all kinds of machines and got furious at my husband, myself, and the crappy situation I found myself in. I was so angry; not only did he destroy our family, but now I was going to let his actions kill me, too? "Screw this." With the same determination I had which had me leave the ICU after my experience with the deadly disease peritonitis, I was determined to move past this ... but I had no idea how. I realized that something had to change, and that was me. I always put myself last. I never took my needs seriously. So that was it ... now, it's my turn.

That's when I enrolled in the PhD program. While I felt so intuitively guided to make that big decision, I was now adding even more stress, expense, and commitments to my already overloaded schedule. I didn't care. It felt like the first time I made a decision based on what I wanted, and as terrifying as it was, it felt good.

This big step was probably the reason why I didn't stay in Stage Three for long. I had a new interest, a new undertaking, and a new desire pulling me forward. I vowed that, *if I can heal from this, I'm taking everyone with me,* and that declaration stoked the flame even more. I was still struggling, but somehow, my pain now had a purpose bigger than me.

Stage Four: Finding and Adjusting to a New Normal

I was soon in a rhythm, and life was getting a bit easier. The pain was still excruciating, but journaling, meditating, conducting my study, and writing my dissertation helped. I was seeing firsthand how people move through this particular type of trauma, and I was implementing everything I was learning. Triggers weren't taking me down like they had in the past, and a new level of confidence was slowly growing. Every tiny achievement in the right direction felt like a sign of progress.

I was figuring out who I wanted to be now with this new experience to move through. I was still in full action mode, except the actions weren't just helping me to survive. Now they were deliberate and intentional—things I was implementing to see what would help. My husband was changing dramatically on his end, too, and while his changes were obvious to anyone who knew him, I was busy creating a new and improved me. The kids were doing well, and we were settling into this new space, slowly but surely.

Stage Five: Healing, Rebirth, and a New Worldview

With a relentless determination to keep moving forward, I was becoming someone I barely recognized. Sure, I kept the parts of me I liked, but a new strength, confidence, and passion was emerging. My heart was slowly beginning to heal; I'd become much more empathetic and compassionate. The three discoveries fueled a new mission to open **The PBT Institut**e thepbtinstitute.com where we could help countless others heal. I did two TEDx talks (Stop Sabotaging Yourself: www.youtube.com/watch?v=XX30i6nC7ro and Do You Have Post Betrayal Syndrome? www.youtube.com/watch?v=iyqOR69dHiU , wrote **The Unshakable Woman** www.amazon.com/Unshakable-Woman-Steps-Rebuilding-Crisis/dp/1543050840 **The Unshakable Woman – the Workbook** www.amazon.com/Unshakable-Woman-Dr-Debi-Silber/dp/1546953639 and **Trust Again** thepbtinstitute.com/trustagain. I started the **From Betrayal to Breakthrough** podcast thepbtinstitute.com/podcast, and at the same time, moved from sadness, to anger, to pity, and toward compassion. I forgave my husband. I shocked myself that I'd even be willing to consider *talking* to him again, let alone *marry* him again. This time, as two completely rebuilt people with new rings, new vows, a new wedding dress, and our four kids as our bridal party.

My heart kept opening, and I interacted with a new level of compassion and love. The little things mattered more than ever, and I felt more gratitude and joy than I'd ever felt before. From this place, the future looks bright, regardless of what direction it takes. I'm trusting that whatever happens is for my highest good, even if it's painful at the time. I'm understanding that we're all doing the best we can, that life is short, that time flies, and that life is precious.

What Stage Are You In?

Do any of the stories shared resonate with you? Have you found yourself in a similar situation, and did you get stuck in any one of those stages? Even if your experience was different, can you see how you may have landed and stayed in a particular stage?

Let's dive into a few tactical tools and strategies you may want to integrate into your routine. Everyone finds what works best for them, so there's no right or wrong here. It's all about being open to exploring some ideas, and then giving them a try and seeing how they make you feel. Some may not make much of an impact, while there may be others that dramatically change your viewpoint, your belief system, and more. When the beliefs change, the body follows, so these changes can also positively impact your health and well-being.

Taking these changes a step further, they also change the quality of your relationships, because you're upgrading how you feel about yourself. When you feel better about yourself, you simply don't tolerate what you may have tolerated when you didn't feel confident, worthy, or deserving. So, let's take a look at a few strategies that may be exactly what you personally need to discover the new 2.0 version of you. Once you choose the one or two that feel like the perfect fit, we'll create a plan to ensure these healing tools become a regular part of your routine. Of course, support and accountability are important, too, so we'll need to make sure they're part of your healing plan.

A Few Tools and Resources

Essential oils:

What are essential oils? The oils extracted and distilled from flowers, plants, herbs, fruits, and vegetables. These oils have a variety of fragrances and aromatic compounds and provide a wide variety of purposes to help with mental, emotional, and physical symptoms. Each compound has unique molecules that offer different benefits. Depending on the particular essential oil and quality of the oil, they can be used topically and/or internally, or they can be diffused. There's such a range in quality, purity, and concentration of an oil based on when and where it's been harvested, how it's been distilled, and other factors.

Many of the products we use every day for our hair, makeup, and skin as well as supplements and cleaning products are filled with toxins and synthetics that cause additional stress on our bodies. As they penetrate into our organs and systems, they create a toxic buildup, which impacts our health, energy, and the way our bodies look and feel.

The uses of essential oils are so widespread and can be used for anything from healthier alternatives to your current cleaning products to boosting the flavors of your favorite foods, to improving physical, mental, and emotional symptoms. For example, some physical symptoms essential oils can help with would be healthier hair and skin, reduced cellular aging, improved sleep, weight loss, digestive issues, headaches, immune support, enhanced energy, and adrenal function, to name a few.

Used for mental and emotional support, certain essential oils help promote a greater sense of calm, clarity, joy, motivation, and hope. They can even offer support when you're working through forgiveness, loss, grief, and so much more.

Here's why I love essential oils thepbtinstitute.com/healing-products/essential-oils:

Let's face it—doing deep-dive work to undo long-standing habits and behaviors is hard work. Or maybe you're working through new emotions based on a recent challenge or experience. Of course, facing those feelings is the only way to truly move through them. However, if you can smell, apply, use, or diffuse an essential oil that can support or accelerate the work you're doing, why not take advantage of that additional help?

I put this idea to the test when I was healing from my betrayal. I remember starting slowly by diffusing scents that simply smelled great without having any idea of what they were doing for me. Since getting a good night's sleep was one of my biggest challenges, I started diffusing lavender and an oil I love called Serenity thepbtinstitute.com/healing-products/essential-oils at night, because they're designed to help improve the quality of your sleep. It helped, so I began to look into a few oils that may help with the wild range of emotions I'd been experiencing like anger, sadness, frustration, hopelessness, and helplessness, to name a few. Some I would diffuse, some I would put on various pulse points (such as behind the ears, wrist, and bottoms of my feet), some I would put on my hands and breathe in deeply, and some I would add to whatever moisturizer I was using. I don't know for sure which oil had the greatest impact, but the overall new self-care routine definitely helped ease some of the painful emotions I'd been experiencing, and I've been using them daily ever since.

I've also learned to use essential oils to help create a mood I'm trying to experience. For example, if I'm about to speak, I'll use an oil to help stay calm or boost motivation. If I'm seeing a friend, I'll often take a deep inhale of an oil that'll help me elevate my mood even more, so I'm sure to bring all I can to our time together. If I'm feeling tired, I'll take a great big sniff of something to give me more energy, and if I'm wired and looking to relax, I'll choose an oil that has a more calming effect. There are so many symptoms essential oils can help with and so many ways to use them. If this feels like a lot, start slowly, and take it from there.

Meditation

Countless studies have proven the health and wellness benefits of meditation. As many studies as there are, there are also countless ways to meditate. Here's where it's helpful to try a few methods and see which resonate best with you.

Would a guided meditation help, where you're being gently led to breathe deeply and envision a certain scene? Would a mantra help that you can repeat as you slowly inhale and exhale? Would a more active type of meditation help, like a walking meditation, where each rhythmic step helps you calm and relax yourself?

What about a body scan where you slowly tense and release muscles from your head to your toes? Or a grounding meditation, where you envision deep roots grounding you to the earth and connecting you from above? What about a healing meditation, where a physical issue is met with a brightly colored energy, enveloping the challenged organ, system, or body part with love and healing? Or would simply focusing on your breath help? For this type of meditation, you mindfully focus on a slow and deep breath as you fill your lungs and expand your belly; then, slowly let it out as you imagine releasing your troubles and pain. Finally, what about picturing taking all of your stress, negative beliefs, old traumas, and painful exchanges and imagining putting them all in a huge garbage bin for the local sanitation crew to pick up?

There are so many ways to meditate, and they don't require sitting on a mountaintop for hours. Even just a few slow and mindful minutes can calm your nervous system, reduce your level of stress, and get you centered and ready for a great day.

Journaling

This one is a personal favorite, and my fellow Type A friends may be able to appreciate why. For me, meditating is great, but sometimes, I don't feel like I'm really doing anything, and I can't tell if I'm doing it "right." Journaling gives me that confirmation, because I feel like I'm actively doing something while also accessing thoughts and behaviors hiding in my subconscious directly under the surface.

Just like with meditation, there are so many ways to journal, too. You can use journal prompts to help open your mind to see something that may be lurking out of reach. Asking journal questions like: "What do I need to know today?" "What do I need to see?" "What am I feeling?" "What do I really want?" can all be great places to start. Without any judgment or agenda, these prompts can often uncover something out of your conscious awareness.

You can also have a dialogue with yourself and a higher power. Whether for you that's God, the Universe, Source, the Divine, Your

Highest Self, Your Intuition, or whatever works for you, initiating a conversation is like improv with the unknown.

I love this model, and it's fascinating to watch the conversation unfold, especially if you really come at this from a place of surrender and letting go. Don't try to steer the conversation or have any expectation of what may show up on the pages of your journal. Just write a dialogue that looks something like this (let's say I'm dialoging with God, so we'll use D for Debi and G for God):

D: I'm frustrated

G: Why?

D: Nothing is working the way I want it to

G: Really? Tell me more about it

D: Deals are falling through, I'm sick of waiting for things, and it's just hard

G: Did you request a certain timeline I'm unaware of?

D: Lol, no, I know I don't have patience, but it feels like I'm waiting all the time for everything

G: Did you wait a long time for that opportunity that happened last week?

D: No, but still

G: If you really looked back over the last month, would you still believe you're waiting a long time for things?

D: Maybe not

G: So what would happen if you allowed for more time for things to unfold, possibly so even bigger and better things have a chance to be orchestrated on your behalf?

D: That would be great

G: Ok, so can you agree to appreciate the process and give yourself more time to watch my magic unfold?

D: Of course. Thank you.

G: You got it

See what I mean? Use whatever or whoever resonates in whatever personality style works for you. I like to keep it friendly and encouraging versus harsh or critical. It's been this style and through writing prompts that I've been able to uncover some of my greatest lessons in life. Want to give it a try?

Here's another idea you may like: You can try free-flow journaling, where you put pen to paper for either a certain length of time or until you've written a certain number of pages. I learned about writing three pages a day from Julia Cameron in her book, *The Artist's Way*. Three pages is a great amount to get the basics out of the way and get to what's lying underneath. Of course, if you're on a roll, don't stop writing. If time is an issue, possibly writing for five or ten minutes a day is a better way for you to go. This way, you're dedicating the time to writing and factoring it into your day at an amount you can maintain.

Have you tried gratitude journaling? They say that committing to writing what you're grateful for each day changes the neurochemistry and wiring of your brain. Gratitude is exceptionally healing, so listing off a few things your grateful for each day can have a positive impact on your outlook on life. What's even better about it is, once you commit to it, you move through your day looking for things you'll be sure to write down when you can. Looking for those things is conditioning your brain in a new way to look for the good versus the bad.

Mindfulness can be exceptionally helpful, too. With mindfulness-based training techniques, you're learning to focus on the present versus the past or the future. Since the present is the only moment we have any control over, focusing on the only moment we can control seems like a healthy idea. There are so many ways to be mindful, and practicing while you eat, move, interact, and do just about anything can help you become so much more fully present and available. With mindfulness, you're training yourself to be less distracted and more present, so you're getting more out of every moment.

Somatic/Body-Based Techniques

There are so many to choose from. The idea is to release the trauma and old beliefs that get stuck within your body and eventually cause symptoms, issues, wear and tear, conditions, and disease. Somatic releasing can be anything from EFT (Emotional Freedom Technique also known as "tapping") to yoga, to Reiki, breathwork, brain spotting, EMDR, dance therapy, and so many more. It would take an entire book just to list them all, and while some methods work wonders for some, others benefit from other approaches. Whether you find a practitioner or implement a strategy you can easily do yourself, the idea is to release the blocked energy that's gotten stuck and has been keeping *you* stuck in the process.

Muscle Testing

What's another interesting way to even know what emotions are trapped in the first place? Muscle testing. Muscles react positively or negatively to the truth. When you're being met with the truth, your muscles will be strong. When you're being told a lie, or when something isn't in your best interest, your muscles will weaken. It's like a handy lie detector test—the "voice of reason" when you're uncertain or unsure.

Just like there are many ways to meditate, journal, or do yoga, there are many ways to muscle test. Here are a few, starting with what I feel is the simplest.: The simplest and most error-proof way I know to muscle test is through the Sway Test, which I learned from Dr. Bradley Nelson, author of *The Emotion Code*. Just like your muscles respond to what's in or not in your best interest, your entire body responds the same way. So to get a sense of what's right, truthful, or in your best interest, you'd stand straight and say something you know for sure is true. You can say your name, the word "love," or envision something that feels good or right to you. Without trying, you'll notice that your body gently sways forward, as if to move toward what you've acknowledged as good, right, or truthful. Then, give yourself a different name, or think of something negative, harsh, critical, or painful. Watch as your body slowly leans back, as if to move away from something negative or uncomfortable. The best part about the sway test is that it's really easy to do. The downside? You can't be so inconspicuous about it. If you're having a conversation and someone is trying to pull a fast one on you, you may feel a bit hesitant to get yourself in the Sway Test stance and lean forward or back based on what they say. I mean, you could, but it would look a little weird.

The next few methods may take some getting used to, but they're equally as effective.

You can muscle test in any way that tests your muscle strength, so here's another way to test: Having your elbows by your side with your forearms at a 90-degree angle, take two fingers from one hand and gently press down on your bent arm as you're testing to see if something is good for you or if something isn't. Your forearm should stay strong if it's good and should be easy to press down if it's not.

Sometimes you may be out and question if a certain food choice or purchase is in your best interest. Here's where you may want to be even more inconspicuous about your truth-telling muscle-testing secret. There are many ways to muscle test. You can create a circle with two fingers on one hand and use a finger of the other hand to test. If the ring created by two fingers of one hand breaks as you try to break it with your finger on the other hand, it's weak, meaning it may not be a fit for you. If the ring remains tight, it may be worth considering.

Of course, I'm taking an entire field of applied kinesiology and giving you the very basics. What I love about muscle testing is it gives you that extra reassurance you need when you're hesitant to make a decision.

Pendulum

The first time someone used a pendulum with me, I thought they were crazy. Now, I see that it's just a physical form of muscle testing and just as effective. What I love about the pendulum is how connected it makes me feel to the unseen when I use it, so I'm going to share what it is, and if it resonates, give it a try.

A pendulum can be as simple as something with weight tied to a string. Or it can be something more ornate and beautiful that even comes in a fancy felt bag. I love them, and while they may seem odd, remember, the more open-minded you are, the more likely you'll move from Willow (Stage Two) to Cactus (Stage Three) to Bamboo (Stage Four) to Lotus (Stage Five), so stay with me.

First, you want to find out how your pendulum lets you know what represents a "yes" and what signifies a "no." So just like with muscle testing, where you ask an obvious question (like your name) to see how it responds, you'll do that with the pendulum, too. I usually put my elbow on the table to steady my arm, holding the pendulum string at the top so it hangs freely. Then, I'll make an obvious statement like, "My name is Debi." It will start to move in a certain direction (for me, it's usually in a straight line up and down) letting me know that up and down signifies a "yes." Then, I'll make another obvious statement I know isn't true like, "My name is Bob." The pendulum will start to move again, this time in a different direction, usually in a circular motion. This motion now represents a "no," which makes sense, since my name isn't Bob. This is how you set up your pendulum, so you'll know what indicates "yes" and "no" responses to the questions you ask.

Next, I'll ask yes or no questions based on what I'm working through. Your questions need to be asked with a "yes" or a "no" response. For example, let's say you're ready and eager to finish a project. Asking a question like, "How long will it take to finish this project?" wouldn't work. Asking something like, "Will I finish this project in less than three months?" would be more effective, because this way, you can get a "yes" or "no" response. I've heard that there are also so many variables when it comes to using a pendulum, including things like travel, sleep, and even dehydration possibly altering results. So, I usually take the time to know for sure what my "yes" and "no" directions are (up and down, circular, etc.) before diving in, and I make sure I'm hydrated and well-rested.

Full credit to my intuitive coach who taught me a pendulum ninja move. I was always wondering if the pendulum could be influenced by what I wanted the outcome to be. For example, if I wanted to know if something was happening soon, I'd use the pendulum, looking for a "yes" or "no," but in all honesty, I was secretly hoping for a "yes." I thought I may be influencing the results, so she taught me another way to use the pendulum, and this may be something you'd like to try, too.

For this other way to use the pendulum, you'll need three or four wipe-off index cards and a dry erase marker. Now, think of a question you want an answer to, and write down three or four possibilities. For example, let's use that same example above—wanting to know if a project was going to be completed soon (assuming you're doing your part in ensuring it gets done). First, test your pendulum, so you know what represents a "yes" and a "no." Then, write a few possibilities on the cards. Maybe on one card, write "less than three months." On another, write "three to six months," on a third card, write "more than six months," and on a fourth card, write "more than one year." Once you've written different possibilities on the cards, shuffle them face down, so you don't know what's written on the different cards. Then, place them all face down in a row without having any idea of which card is in what order. For example, your first card face down may be the card on which you wrote "more than six months," and the next card face down may be the one on which you wrote down "more than one year," and the next one may be the one that says "less than three months." You get the idea.

Now, with the cards written with different possibilities all face down so you have no idea what's written on each, hold the pendulum over each card and see how it moves. In this case, where there are four cards, it's likely you'll get three "no" responses (for me, that would mean circular), and there will be one card where you'll get a "yes" (in my case, that would be up and down, but again, you need to see what a "yes" looks like for you). Once you get your answers, flip over the card that gave you a "yes" response, and voila! Even if you don't agree with pendulums or think it's crazy, at the very least, it's fun, so have an open mind and give it a try.

Strategies and Structure

So now that you have a few options to detect and release trapped emotions and get the answers you're looking for, it's time to incorporate these tools into your daily routine. What I've found is that it's similar to exercise. If you don't work out all week and then hit the gym hard one day, it'll take you days to recover from the muscle soreness, and you're unlikely to want to do that again any time soon. So, it's better to create a plan where you're going for consistency. For that, a few things to consider:

First, let's choose a time during the day. Personally, the morning works best for me, because if it's not done early, there's a good chance it can get knocked off the list if something else needs to get done. Early mornings for many people is a quiet and sacred time that can work, so maybe it'll work for you, too. What I personally like about the morning is that it sets the tone for the day. Wake up rushed and frazzled, and the day will likely be a continuation of the same. Wake up and take time to get calm, grounded, and centered, and it's more likely you'll carry that feeling into your day.

If you're not a morning person, this may take time to get used to, but even getting up a little earlier may be the best way for you to carve out time for your self-care. For others, the end of the day is a great time, and that's fine, too. It's a way to unload everything the day created and help prepare you for a good night's sleep. What's great about a nighttime ritual is that the more calm and centered you feel going to sleep, the more likely you are to have a restful night. Think about it. Having seven or eight hours to marinate over your gratitude list can be very different from seven to eight hours to marinate over stress, trauma, and aggravation.

Once you've figured out the best time for you to create your routine, decide how long you'll devote to your new morning practice. For some, a few minutes each day is all the time they're able to devote, and that's perfectly ok. Maybe dedicating a few minutes each day and a bit longer on the weekends works for you. There's no right or wrong here. You're going for consistency, and it's more effective to do something small each day and then something that requires a long time only once a week.

Once you've decided on something that's a manageable amount of time for you, choose how you want to spend that time. For example, let's say you decide that mornings work for you, and you can easily dedicate five minutes to your new routine Monday through Friday.

On the weekend, you'd like to devote a bit more time, so your routine can look something like this:

From Monday through Friday, you're waking up at 6:55 instead of your usual 7:00 a.m. You're going to roll out of bed, sit in a quiet space, and take a few long, deep breaths as you write down ten things you're grateful for while breathing in some beautifully scented essential oil. On the weekend, you're going to listen to a meditation or take a yoga class.

Here's another example:

If nighttime works better for you, from Monday through Friday, you're going to make sure you shut off all technology at 9:45 p.m. versus 10:00 p.m. like you may usually do. From 9:45 p.m. to 10:00 p.m., you're going to journal a few pages, listen to a guided meditation, read something that helps you feel connected and centered, and then slowly drift off to sleep. On the weekend, maybe you try EFT (tapping), listen to or read a book on mindfulness, or schedule an appointment with a Reiki practitioner.

Creating a routine along with what it entails doesn't have to be rigid and inflexible. The whole idea is to find what it is that works best for you, and integrate it into your routine and life.

Support

Now, let's talk about support. Anything new requires a plan, and that may include the support of others. Do you need to let your family know you're unavailable early in the morning or late in the evening? Do you have a quiet space where you can let others know not to disturb you when you're there? Is there a group you can join for accountability like The PBT Institute thepbtinstitute.com/join or another as you create your new, healthy habits?

You'll likely need to prepare yourself and others as you embark on your new changes. Why? Because just like you've gotten used to your old routine, so did those around you. Now that you're creating these new changes, everyone may need to adjust. Some may have no problem with it, but others might … and that's normal. This happens for a few reasons.

First, many of us don't like change and don't embrace it. We like when things are predictable and when we know what to expect. Your new routine may lead to changes those around you didn't want or expect, so they're hesitant.

I've seen this often, too. Your changes show others what they're unable or unwilling to do. For example, let's say you embark on a healthy eating plan. Your former "food buddies" are now forced to face the fact that they're unwilling to do the same. You're not trying to make them feel bad, but your new desire to become healthy shows them that they're not.

Your changes can also make others uncomfortable because they fear abandonment. I know it sounds harsh, but let's use that same example of adopting new, healthy habits. Your food buddy may be worried you're leaving them behind now that you no longer have your old routine in common. You're ready for the change, but that doesn't mean they are.

How you'd prepare for any change is how you need to plan for support. Letting others know how they can support you, while also letting them know your intentions, can make for a smoother process. It's often the unknown that worries people the most. So, instead of others fearing your changes, see if it is helpful to speak about them, especially if those changes can help them or the relationship. For example, will adopting your new morning routine give you more patience with your kids? Let them know, and they'll likely be more supportive.

Asking and seeking support can also help you stay accountable. If you've asked your family to support you in ensuring you get that morning routine in, and they see you scrolling your social media accounts, it'll help you get and stay on track. If you join a group, and they're expecting you, you're less likely to skip it to do something else.

So now that you have a few tools and strategies, ideas of when to implement them, and ideas on setting up your support system to ensure it gets done, it's time to commit.

I Declare ...

For years, I'd add things to my calendar and send reminders to my phone to make sure I stayed on track. When I *really* didn't trust myself that I'd follow through, I'd make a bold declaration I'd share with others. This was powerful, because once you say it out loud, it's hard to take it back. A declaration comes to mind that I'm sure I would have bailed from had I not declared it out loud.

It was back in my early days as a personal trainer. I had one client who was working with me because she wanted to regain her strength after a recent bout with cancer. She'd been a runner and had lost so much strength and energy, walking around her house was challenging. She had three kids. As hard as it was to be there for them during this time, one of her children had what she called "hysterical paralysis." He couldn't walk once she became sick, and the only explanation they could come up with was that the fear he felt about his mom's illness was behind it.

I started her on a simple walking routine. She'd walk, catch her breath, and begin again. Over time, she wouldn't need the breathing breaks, and she was able to walk without stopping. Next, I added in a short jog. She'd jog, recover, jog again, recover, etc. Eventually, she didn't need the recovery time. She was able to jog without stopping.

One day, I told her that she was ready to run in a 5k. I really wanted her to run in that race as her way of showing herself "she was back." She was strong and able to take on a challenge. She was hesitant, because it felt like a stretch she wasn't sure she'd be able to do. So, as a way of encouraging her to say "yes," I blurted out these words before I could even stop myself:

If you finish, I'll win.

WTH did I just say?? I'd never run in a race, but I saw what her bout with cancer did to her health and self-esteem, and I wanted her to show it who's boss. She looked at me like I was crazy. I had no choice; it was declared.

The day of the race came. We met before the race, gave each other a hug, and I told her I'd be waiting for her at the finish line. How the heck was I going to win this race? There were so many people there! The gun went off, and I took off as if I were on fire. I had no idea what I was doing (probably a good thing), and I ran as if HER life depended on it. She was the only person I thought of as I ran like a crazy person from start to finish. My lungs were burning, and I thought I was going to pass out. I just kept thinking about her and somehow tied my speed to her health. The faster I ran, the healthier she was, and the more certain it was that her cancer was a thing of the past.

I won the race. Not overall, but for my age group, which was still pretty crazy. Now, while this story is to give an example of how declarations ensure you do something, this was one of the most inspiring moments I've ever witnessed, so I'm going to tell you what happened next.

As promised, I waited at the finish line. I waited and waited. I started thinking, "Oh no. I pushed her too hard. She's struggling … why did I ask her to do this in the first place? I'm such an idiot! My job was to just be her trainer. This was too much for her. What was I thinking?" I still waited, hoping she'd cross the finish line any minute. I only had my two older kids at the time, and they'd come to the race with my husband. They were getting restless and wanted to leave. I needed to make sure she finished. More time passed, and I still didn't see her. When it seemed like she wasn't going to cross the finish line, I witnessed the most beautiful sight I'd ever seen …

She slowly walked across the finish line.

While that was an amazing sight to see, what happened next brought me to tears.

Who ran up to give her the biggest hug? Her son, who could suddenly walk again.

The power of a declaration and commitment is so strong. Just as winning the race never would have been possible without my declaration, finishing the race may not have been possible without hers. Just as I ran for her, I'm sure she ran for her son. Whatever your motivation is, see if a declaration can ensure you get the job done.

Connecting with the Wise and Healed Version of You

So now that you have some ideas, some structure, support, and possibly a declaration to make sure it gets done, where do you go from here?

I invite you to meet the wise, strong, empowered version of yourself. The one who's been through it all and has learned so much in the process. The version of you who never would have had the opportunity to be birthed, if you didn't have those painful experiences.

To meet your highest self, close your eyes and get a real sense of who that version of you is. What are the qualities and characteristics? From this healed place, what's different about your demeanor? What's different about the way you speak, think, act, and react? How do you move through your day? What do you do, and who do you spend your time with?

Now get a sense of how you look, how you spend your time, and what you've let go of to be this happy, whole, and confident person. Get a bold and clear picture in your mind. Make it bright and bold, leaving no details behind.

See yourself clearly? Now, seeing this version of you with clarity, walk up to "you" and ask a deeply personal question you want to know. Maybe ask one of the following: "What do I need to do to be as happy as you?" "What have I let go of to enjoy life like you are?" "How did I finally manage to forgive?" Ask your questions, and then tune into your heart and listen for an answer.

Then, ask more questions, including one that'll move you closer to that empowered and enlightened version of yourself you see. Maybe ask: "What's the first thing I need to do?" Or "What's my next step?" Wait for your answer.

Once you've received your answers, thank your wise self for giving you that profound insight. Seal the connection with a long and heartfelt hug. Then, ask how to stay in touch, so you can access their wisdom when you need it again. Listen for the response, feel that connection, and trust the answers you receive.

That version of you is always available. All you need to do is tap into that energy to feel that presence, support, and love. That's who you really are. That's you without the limiting beliefs, outdated ideas, lack mentality, or whatever it is you're working toward letting go of. That's the version of you who knows you best—your wise inner guide you can always trust. The voice of reason, the love you always hoped for, the insight you crave. While it may be the first time you heard from this version of yourself, it's worth strengthening. Why?

It's your best friend.

Your Sticky-Note Self

Sometimes, when I see people who've been through lots of hardship or who have lots of limiting beliefs which have created levels of health, relationships, and finances they're not happy with, I see a very specific scene. I see them covered from head to toe in sticky notes. Let me explain.

Imagine if every time you had a negative belief or assumption about yourself, you wrote it on a sticky note and stuck it somewhere on your body. Maybe you woke up one day, looked in the mirror, and said, "I'm so fat." Imagine writing that on a sticky note and sticking it on your belly. Maybe you had an uncomfortable exchange with someone, and you left the conversation feeling like, "No one understands me." Now imagine writing it on a sticky note and sticking it on your forehead. Maybe you swore you'd stop drinking, bingeing, hitting the snooze button, or whatever habit you were trying to get rid of. You find yourself doing it again and again, although you swore you never would. You call yourself a loser. Write that on a sticky note and stick it on one of your arms. Maybe you've been betrayed. Your trust was shattered, and you don't know how to move forward. You're bitter and resentful. You come out of the experience certain that no one can be trusted. You write a sticky note saying, "Everyone breaks promises" and stick it on your cheek. You get the idea.

Over time, if we kept all those beliefs, assumptions, ideas, and pain from our past experiences with us, we'd be covered from head to toe in sticky notes. We wouldn't even know we have them all over us, because it's something we've gotten so used to, we don't even know they're there.

So how many sticky notes do you carry on you? How long have they been there, and if you were to read each one today, would they all still be true? *Were they ever really true?*

Here's what I suggest: So often, we look to see what we can do to move forward, and that's great. But there really is no reason to bring with you all of those old, outdated sticky notes as you move toward your new strategy, idea, or venture. You're lugging around what no longer serves you. Instead, what would life look like if you asked yourself what sticky notes you've been carrying and if it's time to let them go?

To do this, visualize yourself covered with sticky notes. Move closer and see just how many sticky notes are all over you. See them clearly. Then, get close enough to see what each sticky note says. As you read each one, ask yourself if you still need to have it stuck to you anymore. If you don't, peel it off and throw it away. Read another one. Do you still need that one and the negative statement it says? If not, peel it off and throw it away.

Do this enough and what you'll find is the most beautiful version of you underneath. One that doesn't have all of that negativity covering you, and instead, is radiant and glowing, because the real you has been freed from all those layers of fear, doubt, insecurity, negativity, pessimism, judgment, blame, shame, guilt, and so much more.

Aren't you awesome?

A Final Thought

I commend you. So many people haven't picked up a book since high school, yet here you are almost at the end of this one. What's even more impressive is that you knew something wasn't working for you, so you took steps to do something about it. Maybe that's not a big deal to you, but in my 30 years in business, I've come to realize that's not what so many people do. Many people find themselves stuck and stay there. They resign themselves to a life they're not happy with where the goal is to get through the day. They complain about what's not working, yet don't make changes in order to have a different result.

Not you.

You know there's more, and you're ready to become that version of you who's been waiting to be discovered. It reminds me of this quote from one of my favorite authors, Og Mandino:

"Most humans, in varying degrees, are already dead. In one way or another they have lost their dreams, their ambitions, their desire for a better life. They have surrendered their fight for self-esteem, and they have compromised their great potential. They have settled for a life of mediocrity, days of despair and nights of tears. They are no more than living deaths confined to cemeteries of their choice. Yet they need not remain in that state. They can be resurrected from their sorry condition. They can each perform the greatest miracle in the world. They can each come back from the dead ..."

— **Og Mandino**, *The Greatest Miracle in the World*

As long as you're alive, you're able to change the trajectory of your life. Don't waste this opportunity because it's hard, it's uncomfortable, others will have to adjust, others won't understand, and/or all the other excuses we use to keep us rooted to a situation that doesn't make us happy. A crisis can serve as the ultimate wakeup call. When we hear that dreaded news, or when information is revealed to us that forever changes life as we've known it, we're shocked and need to figure out a way to survive and move through our experiences. I talk about the two types of crises that move us toward action in my book, **The Unshakable Woman** www.amazon.com/Unshakable-Woman-Steps-Rebuilding-Crisis/dp/1543050840. There's the life crisis (death of a loved one, disease, devastation of some kind like abuse, betrayal, financial crisis, etc.). Then there's what I call the self-induced life crisis. This is the one where we've had it with our current scenarios and lifestyle.

With a self-induced life crisis, we make a decision. Here's the day you throw out the cookies, make the doctor's appointment, quit the job, join the gym, have that difficult conversation, or throw away the alcohol. Here's where you've had enough of your excuses and the results they've brought you. Here's where change begins. Everyone around you can see that there's a resolve, a strength, a force that's just begun. There's a flame lit from within, and you're different. You're unwilling to get caught up in your reasons, your story, your justifications, and everything you've told yourself that's been keeping you stuck. You've outgrown that story and all it has brought you. You're not quite sure what's ahead, but you know you're ready to find out. You're scared, but you're ready to venture into this new space. You're tired of putting your needs and passions on the back burner. You realize that your needs are just as important as everyone else's, and it's time to prioritize them.

As this flame within begins to take hold, it moves you forward. The path is unsteady and unpredictable, but intuition and your highest self are guiding you along the way. You're less interested in what your ego is saying as you listen to the gentle guidance of your Highest Self instead. You take a deep breath, trust, and allow for changes to unfold. It's an unfamiliar space, but a growing level of self-trust is giving you the assurance you need to know you're on the right track. There's no confirmation yet; it's like trying to see through the fog, but each step clears your vision and confirms you're on the right path.

As scary as it is, confidence builds, and now you're excited about where you're headed. It's still unclear, but it's better than where you've been. Maybe you find some like-minded soul warriors also headed for growth. The conversations are different. You're not talking about the mundane; you're talking about the possibility. You're not complaining about the past; you're excited about the future. You're not wishing it were different; you're actively creating something better. Sure, you're going to stumble and fall, but each time you get up, it's another sign that you trust the process; you trust yourself, and you keep going. Not exactly sure where you're headed, it's terrifying yet exciting. Some will understand, others won't, and that's ok. With love and compassion, you realize you don't have to explain yourself, make excuses for yourself, or justify why you want something. Your soul is on fire, and only those on a similar path will understand. When you run into those people, you'll know it instantly. The conversations are different. You'll notice that these types of conversations give you energy versus drain you. You'll leave interactions like this with more energy and ideas than you had before you met with this fellow soul warrior. You'll be eager to keep going, and as you do, some will think you're crazy, and others will be inspired by who you're becoming.

Don't stop. Every single human being on this planet has a unique strength, gift, talent, and calling. While some of us know what that is from the time we're very young, so many others discover it through hard times, crises, trauma, and the most challenging times in life. Let them take you down, and you'll have your story of lack and scarcity. Use them as the launchpad for transformation, and you become a force of nature. It's not in some of us; it's available to us all. Whether it's the life crisis, or the self-induced life crisis, they're both incredible opportunities if we allow them to be.

With the life crisis, you've been through the worst of it already. Don't you owe it to yourself to do something good with something bad? With the self-induced life crisis, don't you want to see how you took control of your thoughts, behaviors, and beliefs and told them who's boss as you created a version of yourself you're proud of?

It's time. How great would it be if at the end of our journeys, instead of talking about all we didn't do, we talk about how exciting of a ride it was? Instead of talking about "I wish I ..." "I should have

..." and "If only ..." we have a different conversation. What if we talked about how scary it was, but in those bold moves we took, we created something wonderful? Maybe an outrageous experience, a legacy business, or a fantastic family adventure. What if you created the body and health you always dreamed of? What if you dared to be bold enough to go for it, and because you did, you're living that life you thought was only reserved for others? One filled with love, meaning, and purpose? What if the only thing stopping you is the self-talk between your ears convincing you that it's only reserved for others? What if you told that voice that you're done having it live rent-free in your mind? What if you realized you have everything you need, and you're ready for more?

These are my favorite conversations—those all about possibility and the hero's/heroine's journey. My plan? When I turn 90 years old, I'm changing my business model. I guess it'll be time to slow down a little. By that time, it will be by 65th year in business, working with hundreds of thousands of incredible people if not more. I'll be hosting sunset happy hours on my beautiful patio overlooking the ocean meeting from Monday through Friday with everyone whose life I somehow touched and who made the decision to create a life of meaning and significance.

Appointments will need to be scheduled far in advance because of how many people there will be to meet with. These appointments, once scheduled, are two hours each, so we're not rushed. I'll be meeting with only one person at a time, to enjoy you, your story of triumph, and that particular sunset we'll enjoy together. Here's how I see it:

You'll be welcomed into my beautiful home I'll be living in then, greeted with a heartfelt hug, and I'll walk you to the patio, where you'll sit in a comfortable lounge chair, and I'll sit in another. You'll tell me all about your journey: the highs, the lows, the challenges, and the triumphs as we hear the waves crashing and watch the sun set on another beautiful day. We'll laugh like kids, the snorty kind of laughter, as you share what a wild ride you've had. As the sun sets on that magnificent day, together we'll appreciate the road you traveled while creating your legacy of love, meaning, contribution, and significance.

I'll have decadent and delicious snacks ready (by 90, I've earned the right to eat whatever I want, right?), and you'll bring the pictures and journals, so you don't leave out a detail. You'll need them as reminders, so you can easily recount the whole exciting journey.

Your journey has begun, and I can't wait to meet with you in person and hear your whole story, firsthand. See you then!

Next Steps

So, where do you go from here? This is always a bittersweet part of writing for me. We've just gotten to know each other, and now we're at the end of the book! Since I'm really bad at saying "goodbye," here are a few ways we can continue to stay in touch:

If I can put my 30 years of coaching to use in order to work personally with you and ensure you become the Bamboo or Lotus you're meant to be, reach out to ClientCare@PBTInstitute.com.

If you feel you're more like the Willow or Cactus, let's get you the exact support you need. For that, start by taking the **Healed or Hardened Quiz** HealedOrHardenedQuiz.com to be sure where you land for your best next steps.

If membership within The PBT Institute is right for you, learn more about it here: thepbtinstitute.com/join.

For Trust Again: Overcoming Betrayal and Regaining Health, Confidence and Happiness, get it along with lots of goodies here: thepbtinstitute.com/trustagain.

Interested in becoming a coach like Elizabeth, Josh, and Michelle?

Learn more about becoming a Certified PBT Coach or Practitioner here: thepbtinstitute.com/certification.

Never miss an episode by subscribing to the free and info-packed *From Betrayal to Breakthrough* podcast where twice each week, I'm bringing you tons of amazing guests and information: thepbtinstitute.com/podcast.

Stay in touch on social and other links you may enjoy:

The site: thepbtinstitute.com

The latest TEDx: "Do You Have Post Betrayal Syndrome?": www.youtube.com/watch?v=iyqOR69dHiU

TEDx: Stop Sabotaging Yourself: www.youtube.com/watch?v=XX30i6nC7ro

Facebook: www.facebook.com/InspireEmpowerTransform

Twitter: twitter.com/DebiSilber

Linkedin: www.linkedin.com/in/debisilber

Instagram: www.instagram.com/debisilber

Youtube: www.youtube.com/debisilber

About the Author

Debi Silber, PhD, Founder and CEO of the PBT (Post Betrayal Transformation) Institute (ThePBTInstitute.com), is a holistic psychologist and a health, mindset, and personal development expert. She is an award-winning speaker, keynoting events such as the Women's Summit at Bryant University, the American Heart Association's Go Red event, the Women's Leadership Conference, MGM Grand, and many more.

Dr. Silber is a two-time TEDx speaker, has contributed articles and insights to *The Dr. Oz Show, Fox, CBS, News12, multiple times to the Huffington Post, Forbes, Shape, Self, WebMD, Working Mother, Glamour, Ladies Home Journal, Women's World, MSN, and YahooShine*, to name a few. She was a featured expert on the local CBS affiliate show *Live It Up* and on websites such as Working Mother, Medium, and Thrive Global. She has been featured as a self-improvement expert in four books, including *Power Moms: The New Rules for Engaging Mom Influencers Who Drive Brand Choice*, and was even profiled in the textbook *Exploring Global Issues: Social, Economic, and Environmental Interconnections*, which aims to inspire students to pursue similar careers. She is also host of the podcast, **From Betrayal to Breakthrough,** and is a popular podcast, virtual summit, and media guest.

A holistic registered dietitian with a master's degree in nutrition, a certified personal trainer, and a Whole Health Coach™, she has two certifications in pre- and postnatal fitness with specialty recognition in weight loss and weight maintenance. Debi is a functional diagnostic nutritionist and has just completed her PhD in transpersonal psychology (the psychology of transformation and human potential), for which she conducted a groundbreaking study on how we experience betrayal— what holds us back and what helps us heal. She has achieved various honors, such as winning the 2018 Future of Health award, where her discoveries on betrayal were voted on and recognized by more than 500 health and wellness professionals; the 2017 Long Island Business News Award-Achievements in Health Care; Health Tap's 2015 Nutrition Industry winner; 2014 Top Ranked U.S. Executive by the National Council of American Executives; and a Notable American Woman.

She's the author of the several books, including *Trust Again: Overcoming Betrayal and Regaining Health, Confidence and Happiness* (Roman & Littlefield), *The Unshakable Woman: 4 Steps to Rebuilding Your Body, Mind and Life after a Life Crisis* (Createspace, foreword by J. J. Virgin), *The Unshakable Woman—The Workbook*

(Createspace); *The Lifestyle Fitness Program: A Six Part Plan So Every Mom Can Look, Feel and Live Her Best* (Morgan James, recommended by Jack Canfield and *Parenting* magazine), and *A Pocket Full of Mojo: 365 Proven Strategies to Create Your Ultimate Body, Mind, Image and Lifestyle* (Createspace, recommended by Brian Tracy and Marshall Goldsmith). *A Pocket Full of Mojo* was purposely written to be sold as a bulk book option to companies serving as a low-investment corporate wellness tool, which she has sold to PayPal, Life Time Fitness clubs, and law and accounting firms.

She's married (twice) to her husband Adam, and they have four children (Dani, Dylan, Camryn, and Cole), two "bonus" daughters (Molly and Keely), and four dogs (Scooby, Gigi, Brody, and Kasey). Debi's greatest passion is helping others become their physical, mental, and emotional best.

Please stay in touch! Join our community thepbtinstitute.com, and share your success! I'd love to hear about your journey, and I know it'll inspire others too.

1   https://www.merriam-webster.com/dictionary/hardened?src=search-dict-box

2   https://www.merriam-webster.com/dictionary/healed

3   https://www.cdc.gov/coronavirus/2019-ncov/daily-life-coping/managing-stress-anxiety.html

4   https://doi.org/10.1093/qjmed/hcaa201

5   https://doi.org/10.1016/j.chiabu.2020.104699

6   https://www.ajemjournal.com/article/S0735-6757(20)30307-7/fulltext#bb0050

7   https://www.ajemjournal.com/article/S0735-6757(20)30307-7/fulltext#bb0060

8   https://doi.org/10.1016/j.chiabu.2020.104699

9   https://doi.org/10.1111/famp.12576

10   https://www.bloomberg.com/news/articles/2020-03-31/divorces-spike-in-china-after-coronavirus-quarantines

Made in the USA
Las Vegas, NV
21 December 2021

39169974R00118